JAYANTA MAHAPATRA

His Mind and Art

JAYANTA MAHAPATRA

His Mind and Art

By

A.A. Khan
Rahul Mene

ADHYAYAN

ADHYAYAN PUBLISHERS & DISTRIBUTORS
NEW DELHI (INDIA)

Published by
ADHYAYAN PUBLISHERS & DISTRIBUTORS
4378/4B, 105, J.M.D House, Murari Lal Street
Ansari Road, Darya Ganj, New Delhi-110 002
Ph: 011- 23263018, 011-23277156, FAX: 011-23280028
E-mail: adhyayanpublishers@yahoo.com

Jayanta Mahatra: His Mind and Art

First Edition 2011

ISBN 978-81-8435-278-8

Printed in India

Published by Harish Chandra Yadav for Adhyayan Publishers & Distributors, Laser Typesetting at A.V. Rao Laser Typesettings, New Delhi and Printed at Tarun Offset Printers, Delhi.

Acknowledgments

We are obliged to the poet Jayanta Mahapatra, for making his poetry available to us and helping us to remain in the right track when we approached him. We wish to acknowledge his support to our approach and insight in grabbling with his apparently simple but complex poetry.

We are also obliged to Dr. Binod Mishra, Assistant Professor in the Department of Humanities and Social Sciences, Indian Institute of Technology, Roorke (Uttarakhand) for his valuable suggestions in carrying on with our work.

We are greatly indebted to acknowledge the cooperation received from Dr. (Mrs.) Qamar Talat, professor, Department of English, Govt.. V.Y.T.P.G. Autonomous College, Durg (C.G.) for her constant support and encouragement.

We place our thanks to Adhyayan Publishers and Distributors, New Delhi for readily accepting to publish this book in such a short time and in such a nice form.

Dr. A.A. Khan

Dr. Rahul Mene

Preface

To see a World in a Grain of Sand
And a Heaven in a Wild Flower,
Hold Infinity in the palm of your hand
And Eternity in an hour.
Lines from "Auguries of Innocence", Blake. William)

Jayanta Mahapatra (1928-) is one of the best known Indian English poets. He also writes in Oriya. Mahapatra was born in 1928 in Cuttack, the city where he spent most of his lifetime. He has worked as a lecturer in Physics at a succession of colleges chiefly in the Orissa region including Ravenshaw College, Cuttack. He retired in 1986. Mahapatra has authored eighteen volumes of poetry(to date, including his *Selected Poems*), five volumes of Oriya poetry, eight volumes of poetry translations from Oriya to English, two volumes of stories, one book on Orissa and many articles in various journals, periodicals and newspapers. Mahapatra is a Sahithya Akademi awardee, and also a recipient of the Jacob Glatstein award conferred by Poetry magazine, Chicago. Besides poetry, he has experimented widely with myriad forms of prose. Mahapatra is also a distinguished editor and has been bringing out, for many years, a literary magazine, Chandrabhaga, from Cuttack. The magazine is named after Chandrabhaga, a prominent river in Orissa.

By all standards, Mahapatra's tryst with the muse came rather late in life. He took to writing poetry when he was into his 40s. The publication of his first book of poems, Svayamvara and Other Poems, in 1971 was followed by the publication of Close the Sky, Ten by Ten. One of Mahapatra's better remembered works is the long poem Relationship, for which he won the Sahitya Akademi award in 1981. He is the first Indian English Poet to bag the honour. Besides being one of the most popular Indian poets of his generation, Mahapatra was also part of the trio of poets who laid the foundations of Indian English Poetry. He shared a special bond with A. K. Ramanujan, one the finest poets in the Indo English Poetry tradition. Mahapatra is also different in not being a product of the Bombay school of poets. Over time, he has managed to carve a quiet, tranquil poetic voice of his own—distinctly different from those of his contemporaries. His wordy lyricism combined with authentic Indian themes put him in a league of his own.

Mahapatra was conferred the Padma Shri in 2009 and was awarded an honorary doctorate by Ravenshaw University on 2nd May 2009.

In Mahapatra's poetry, the primacy of reader-response is as much valid as the primacy of the text itself. Mahapatra's poetry does not give any message to its readers in the form of a well-phrased witticism. Instead, it makes the reader look inwards, question himself about life, its significance, uncertainty and so on leading him into a process of personal discovery. This indeed is the greatest strength of Mahapatra's poetry.

Mahapatra has repeatedly and candidly said that when he started writing poetry, his knowledge of poetry did not go beyond a few poems of Wordsworth, Keats and Shelley prescribed in the school syllabus. At heart he is a romantic; only his intellect sharpened by the profession of teaching physics won't let him indulge in it. In his poetry one feels the presence of "the still, sad music of humanity" of Wordsworth, the sweeping lyrical grace of Shelley and the sensuousness of Keats. He has always remained close to the Romantic notion of the poet's inescapable presence in the poem; it nevertheless embodies in such a self a deep subjectivity that sets it apart from contemporary Indian poetry in English. According to Mahapatra, there cannot be any hard and fast rules, but poetry that ignores the historical relationship between the self and the society becomes lifeless. "The poet who does not see reality around himself is dead; so too the poet who 'only' sees reality around him." That is how he deals with the grim realities that surround him and scream for attention.

The book has been divided into seven chapters. The first chapter entitled "Formative Influence" is an attempt to throw light on Mahapatra's indefatigable efforts as the poet "reflects the earth's lost amplitudes." The "lost amplitudes" evoke his sense of retrievability of the Indian past, myth, culture, tradition, legends, rituals, etc. by the means of the poetic art through the English language. For Mahapatra has firm hope and belief in exploitation of the English language. He affirms that his feel for the English words and their sonorous music has affected his temperament and vision. His poetic vision is profoundly shaped by the ambience of Orissa evidenced in temples, architecture and sculptures. His Physics discipline has stood him in good stead in tempering his vision into a well-crafted poetry. Mahapatra's restless preoccupation with his characteristic poetic diction is in its formative stage of his poetry is quiet evident.

The second chapter, "His Philosophical Humanism" intends to record Jayanta Mahapatra as a humanist in the trinity of "religion", "culture" and "time." His 'religion' is a belief in humanistic values; his 'culture' represents refinement of those values; and time-consciousness signifies the complexity of experiences of life and also the present as an interminable extension of the past into future, which is deeply rooted in the past. Moreover, Mahapatra uses certain images and symbols in his poetry like *death, darkness, past, silence, door, etc.,* which become the recurrent motifs of his poetry. Mahapatra's poetry volumes are held in closer relationship by the recurrence of these motifs, as well as by their thematic repetitiveness, which give unity and significance to Mahapatra's modes of perceiving an experience rooted either in the reality of the external world or the interior landscape of his poetic imagination.

The third chapter entitled, "Jayanta Mahapatra – Social Commitment", proposes that Jayanta Mahapatra's poetry is essentially metaphorical in nature. His language of poetry depicts the socio-cultural ambience of Orissa, by the experiencing self of the poet. Naturally, the language becomes resonant, sophisticated and metaphorical by transcending the superficial meanings of the words and thereby becoming an integrated symbol which creates a new poetic stylistics. Moreover, Mahapatra believes that the specificity of Orissan culture itself generates the symbolic modes of perceiving an experience, which come naturally to the poet for whom the landscape is inseparably linked with his destiny, so the metaphoric mode in the image-oriented poetry of Mahapatra becomes the nucleus of his creative endeavours.

It is not surprising that in the highly subjective poetry of Jayanta Mahapatra, ironic mode of expression is neither a dominant nor a preferred poetic device. Infact, in his early poetry, irony is conspicuously absent. Mahapatra plunges into the depths of his own self in his exploratory poetic journey to know himself better. It is only in his recent poetry volumes that we get to see glimpses of Mahapatra's ironic mode at certain social issues when the moral of a society as a whole is at its nadir although, Mahapatra's irony is not a pungent remark or a comment and is never biting, bitter or sharp; it never borders on sarcasm or takes cover under witty statements. Irony in Mahapatra's poetry, when present, is always subdued, almost like a private whisper that invariably leads to self- introspection,. being directed more towards himself, focusing on his own limitations and shortcomings both as man and poet.

"A Missing Person", "Hunger", "The Whorehouse in a Calcutta Street", "30th January 1982: A Story" and "The Twentyfifth Anniversary of a Republic: 1975" are the classic examples of Mahapatra's poetry as social commitment. Here, we may observe how irony, though mute in the characteristic style of Mahapatra, renders an intensity and immediacy to the experience handled in the specific contexts of his poetry. At the same time, the poems lead to the realisation of human predicament entrapped in the complex web of social pressures which, infact, act as serious constraints on the choices open to an individual to lead his life in accordance with his personal preferences.

The fourth chapter, "Jayanta Mahapatra – The Mouth-Piece of India" is an attempt to place Mahapatra to the group of modern experimentalists in Indian English poetry. His works seem to be attempts to link to the kinds of Indian reality. They also express conflicting concerns of modern life partially colouring them with his personal and immediate response to the world unfolding before him. They also seem to be introspections into the customary notion of reality. It appears he conceives a poem as an object having a structure of images and symbols. Images employed in his poems try to bring to the surface his obsessing memories, doubts and experiences which have been the source material of his imagination. He seems to be much intimate to the modernist movement of the first half of the century. The use of recurring symbols and his greater dependence on open-ended literary forms are endeavours to give coherence to non-linear, fragmented structures. Actually Jayanta Mahapatra's poetic art is not for the large masses, but it is meant for a small discriminating readership. Mahapatra's poetry should be evaluated in the perspective of the locale, in terms of the images drawn from the geographical, social and cultural sources of his native land of Orissa. The place with all its ethos and myths, its lives and beliefs, superstitions and transitions has been the governing factor of Mahapatra perceptions and vision.

The fifth chapter, "The Problems of Heritage – Myths, Rites, Rituals" is a study of Mankind who is continually engaged in a fruitful search for the right clues to unravel the mysteries of Nature. Through his varied activities man transforms Nature for making his life more comfortable and in the process he is also simultaneously transformed by Nature which creates a new awareness and also generates new needs and aspirations. Both these transformations are conditioned by the historical and social environments which are operative in the specific contexts of time and place. No man has freedom in the choice of an appropriate time, a suitable place or a favourable socio-historical condition to begin his life simply because he cannot choose his parents. A man is born into a specific socio-cultural milieu and he inherits, quite unconsciously though, and often without efforts, the accumulated wisdom of earlier generations in the form of traditions, legends and myths. Therefore, it is apt to say that "myth is the embodiment of human aspiration and its appropriate imaginative form". Myths are the potent symbols of man's dreams and aspirations, which provide him with ideals and help him set goals in a hostile world that constantly threatens man's existence. Struggle for survival consume man's life energies and he needs fresh impetus to go on facing and tackling the new obstacles which keep propping up like the ending, rolling waves in the sea.

Mahapatra is haunted by a strange sense of fear and uneasiness throughout. In many cases the source of these apprehensive feelings is his own imagination without a correspondence, atleast the obvious one, in the external reality. It looks as though these fears are grounded in the primitive consciousness of the prehistoric man, who being unable to explain the natural phenomena of fire, thunder, lightening, rain, etc., looked at them with awe and wonder. He came to regard these as manipulations of superior astral powers which guided the life and destiny of men and matters alike, the uncertainties of his nomadic life coupled with the equally unpredictable vagaries of Nature, left everything to chance in that primitive society, including man's very own survival. This certainly must have contributed to man's fear of the inexplicable in the universe and perhaps also roused his curiosity to explore, what he might have inferred to be a fundamentally more powerful but equally invisible causative factor. Thus, the primitive man came to believe in the mystery of the universe, driven as he was, by a strong desire to live and propagate. Naturally then he felt the need to appease these *unknown forces* to protect him from their potential destructive powers and also to seek their benediction to live and prosper. Mahapatra narrates the practice of human sacrifice conducted, till the end of the last century, by the Kondhs, a primitive tribal community which inhabits the mountainous tracts of south and west Orissa.

Thus, rituals and magic were devised which represented symbolically man's submission to the superior powers. Conversely, this ritualistic magic also became the means of man's quest to know, understand and interpret the nature of this mysterious power. This is how perhaps religion was born with its intricate system of secret signs and symbols, from the rudiments of man's fear of the inexplicable, the unknown and his curiosity to explore the unknowable. Jayanta Mahapatra makes an attempt to articulate these symbolic gestures of mankind's eternal search into the unknown through his poetry. For Mahapatra, no history of human civilisation will be complete without considering its rites and rituals which bind people together into an identifiable whole, as a community. A deep insight into the natural of these rites becomes compelling as it forms a vital part of the socio-historical background of Orissa.

The sixth chapter entitled, "Growing Materialism and Corruption of Humanity" focuses on growing materialism and corruption of humanity in contemporary life and society as well. He feels agonised about real living of poor people. The poet's anguish is palpable as the life has gone astray with the jungle law. Mahapatra dwells on hunger, violence and terrorism. He judges political issues from the humanistic view point. He depicts the predicament of human life. Mahapatra tries in vain to speak out realities of life in India. He thus tries to identify himself with the complex problems of the society as a humanist. As a modern poet Jayanta Mahapatra tries to 'connect' himself with the contemporary world and he realises that he should be "aware of what's going on around him: the poverty, the greed, the unnecessary violence, the cruelty, the injustice, the sexuality." Man's cruelty to man has become the order of the day. The poet's brio lies in exploiting the day-to-day situations out of the contemporary world. Life in India has drowned headlong in poverty, wretchedness and destitution, the poet says that the heritage of our culture has waned over the centuries and it is understood to be at nadir because of self-centredness of the leaders of the country. Mahapatra casts aspersions on the failure of the government to provide succour to the people in their need. The poet's father is the mouthpiece to vent the poet's feelings of vexation.

The seventh chapter presents the conclusion of the study.

Mahapatra's poetry has a remarkable spontaneity which indicates that poetry comes natural to him as day-dreaming does to an adolescent. His themes are characterised by the private and public, the religious and the metaphysical, the national and the universal, the contemporary and the perennial, superimposed by the hermit-like meditativeness, revealing "a contemplative centrality of vision." But then Mahapatra's poetry does have certain limitations as well. He is prone to thematic repetitiveness, logorrhea, jumbling up numerous ideas in a poem and inelegant patterning of images. However, these demerits notwithstanding, Mahapatra's poetry both in quality as well as quantity, is impressive and refreshing.

Contents

1

Formative Influence

It is a known genetic fact that offsprings from parents of mixed racial parentage are known to have extraordinary and exotic looks. A walk down the corridors of history also shows that, over a period of time, even between conquering and conquered countries, a healthy assimilation of cultures has had a healing effect in normalising relations between the two. Thus, Rome overran Greece, but went on to spread Greek culture throughout the Roman world. The English language itself, represents a marriage of more than one linguistic partner: mainly Anglo-Saxon, Norman-French, with touches of Latin, Gaelic and Celtic words.

It is thus, no surprise that the long connection between India and Britain resulted in the growth of a new literature, which we, today, classify as Indian Writing in English. It owes its origin to Macaulay's "Minutes" in English, no other single document having had a more profound influence on the cultural development of a conquered nation. In times, English became not only the language of administration, but also of creative self- expression - in the vein of the poetry prevalent in England at that time. English was, and still is, the language of an elite, numerically large, yet a smaller proportion of the population as a whole. Arguably if any legacy is left to us by the British, it is English, which has been playing a decisive role in our society.

The Indian subcontinent has come under the influence of various cultures and languages as a result of innumerable invasions by the foreign invaders in their quest for conquering new territories. But, subsequently, all such influences were absorbed by the Indian soil in such a way that they underwent a sea-change and became yet another enrichment of Indian culture. Similarly, English language, too, has now become an integral part of our cultural and social life. The wealth of information and knowledge the language brings with it, have contributed to the forever expanding horizons of our cultural and intellectual pursuits.

The question of creative self-expression, not in the writer's mother-tongue, but in what is apparently an alien language – English – is a sensitive one, generating diverse point of view. Further, if the expression in a language other than his mother-tongue comes easily and naturally to a writer, and he is bilingual without effort, there is no reason why he / she should not write in another language. This is certainly the *care* for the Indian writer in English. In this context, James H. Cousins rightly remarked as early as in 1918, that Indian Writing in English should be "Indian in spirit, Indian in thought, Indian in emotion, Indian in imagery and English only in words."[1]Therefore, it is apt to say that Indianness should permeate all Indian writing in English so as to give it credibility, respectability and an identity of its own.

On the other hand, the place and status of Indian English poetry before and after Independence are open to debate. There are people representing diametrically opposite views on the achievement of this poetry in general. One group out rightly condemns the poetry written before 1947 and eulogises the Post-Independence Indian English poetry. R. Parthasarthy's pronouncement that Indian verse in English, "did not seriously begin to exist till after the withdrawal of the British from India."[2] P. Lal and Adil Jussawalla are in the company of R. Parthasarthy in denouncing the poetry of Sri Aurobindo and his contemporaries.

Whereas, there are critics like V.K. Gokak, C.D. Narasimhaiah and a few others who have lauded the poetry of Sri Aurobindo, Sarojini Naidu and Toru Dutt. To Gokak, Sarojini Naidu is the Yeats of India and Sri Aurobindo a great innovator in the act of Versification. C.D. Narasimhaiah speaks of Toru Dutt, Sarojini Naidu and Sri Aurobindo in admiration in his well known book, *The Swan and the Eagle*. He lauded both Toru and Sarojini as pioneers in the field of Indian English poetry. C.D. Narasimhaiah is more eloquent in his praise of Sri Aurobindo whom he considers not only as a distinguished poet but critic too. He goes a step forward to tell that English language has gained from Sri Aurobindo and compares him with Joseph Conrad who broadened the descriptive range of the English language. He says, "It may be said of Sri Aurobindo that he made the English language accommodate certain hitherto unknown (inconscient) areas of experience both through his prose work, "Life Divine" and through his epic *Savitri*, not to speak of the numerous translations from Sanskrit poetry and drama as well as his other less known but important works."[3]It is interesting and important to remember that Sri Aurobindo nearly succeeded in creating an idiom in English which is peculiar and unique to the genius of Indian people. In the course of an article entitled "Indian poetry in English Yesterday-Today-Tomorrow" (*The Literary Criterion* Vol. XVIII No. 3, 1983 pp. 9-18), well-known scholar and critic K.R.S. Iyenger takes R. Parthasarthy, Keki. N. Daruwalla and Adil Jussawalla to task for criticising Sri Aurobindo and earlier poets in English for wrong reasons.

Post-Independence Indian English poets beginning with Nissim Ezekiel. To some pursuits the best – post – 1947 poets in English would appear as pseudo – Keats, second – rate Tennyson, third – rate Hardy, and forth – rate Eliot. One believe that serious Indian English poetry came to be written not immediately after independence but in the 'Sixties and after. The Indian English poetic movement of the 'Sixties and 'Seventies did much to fix its image as deliberately deficient, moderate with a will. Indian English poets sought comparisons with Anglo-Americans and unfortunately, followed either the genteel English poets and this tendency has gradually frayed and will probably give way altogether for the fact that however deliberate post-Independence Indian English poetry has proved increasingly robust, varied, responsive to the times and enjoyable. It has acquired a distinct character and discovered its own voice. The voice is discovered by the poet's genius for intimately registering the idiom of his own world. Post-Independence Indian English poetry is both a break with the past and a continuation with it too. It tries hard to set its root and develop its own artistic credo. It has successfully risen above "decadent romanticism" and in the hands of such brilliant poets as Nissim Ezekiel, A.K. Ramanujan, and R. Parthasarthy, it is acquiring new dimensions.

Jayanta Mahapatra, A.K. Ramanujan, R. Parthasarthy, Arun Kolatkar and Kamala Das turn inward to get into their roots. There is a need to acclimatize English language to an indigenous tradition to write poetry effectively. For Mahapatra has firm hope and belief in exploitation of the English language. He avowedly says:

> Yes, there is a poem growing
>
> with a foreign language which keeps my head up.[4]
>
> ("Even If No One Takes My Poems Seriously")

R. Parthasarthy, as it were, gives a clarion call to Indian English poets to return to their respective linguistic traditions. He asks:

> How long can foreign poets
>
> Provide the staple of your lines?
>
> Turn inward, scrape the bottom of your past.
>
> (Rough Passage)

Post – Independence Indian English poetry is genuine because it is deeply felt and addressed to the whole community. Indian situations form a vital part of it. It seems natural to conclude that a poet with a live cultural past behind him, aware of his roots and perhaps prejudiced by those roots, has a greater probability of writing significantly than one who has no knowledge of any Indian language other than English. Jayanta Mahapatra's *Relationship* is set in Orissa – a land of "forbidding myth." Mahapatra is "caught in the current of time" and in his attempt to "go into the unknown in me" tries "to speak of the myth of sleep and action / in the hope of soothing myself and those others" have unmistakably indicated the direction Indian English poetry is likely to take in future. The very fact that Jayanta Mahapatra has been consistently bringing out his poetry-volumes is a sure sign of his bubbling creativity and of his firm anchorage in the sphere of the Indian poetry in English. Also, his poetry has been well-received by the reading public, both at home and abroad. The many awards and distinctions that are bestowed on him are a true tribute paid to Mahapatra's poetic talents simultaneously, it tries to view Jayanta Mahapatra in terms of the mythic structure and symbols that shape and control his vision. .

The early period of nineteenth century was of crucial period of our history. It was the period of darkness in all aspects of life. Politically, slave of England; socially, chained with old rottened customs; economically, spoiled by gradual decay of various industries and Nature – dependent agriculture; culturally feeling shameful for past without knowing it. In such a dark period Jayanta Mahapatra was born on 22nd October 1928, in Cuttack, Orissa. Dilly–dallying with photography, he began writing poetry. Born and brought up in Orissa, he might have written in his mother tongue Oriya, though, of course, he did not for several good reasons. Explaining these reasons, he says:

I am in love with English. And then, my schooling

was in English – and I learnt my language from British schoolmasters – mainly from English novels: so blame H. Rider Haggard and Edgar Rice Burroughs and Ballantyne from whom I caught the first delight of words gravid with meaning. Further I feel I can express myself better in English than in Oriya.[5] (59)

Mahapatra was twice removed from his immediate surroundings – first, he was born into a Christian family in a predominantly Hindu society and second, he wrote in an acquired medium, English, which was considered not adequate to encompass the cultural spirit of his native land. Yet the themes which dominate his poetry are related to such stark realities of India as hunger, myths, rituals, sexuality, spirituality, the self and eternity. His poetry, whether describing the locale, its environs and landscape or the relationship of his self to his land, attempts to reflect an awareness of this milieu. It aims at analysing and evaluating the form and vision of his poetry in the perspective of the locale, in terms of the images drawn from the geographical, social and cultural sources of his native land of Orissa. The place with all its ethos and myths, its lives and beliefs, superstitions and transitions has been the governing factor of Mahapatra's perceptions and vision.

Mahapatra's concern with the local emerged gradually as he realised the need of an idiom that would transcend passions and sensuousness into an awareness of the self in search of an identity. He began writing poems as any other poet would. Frustrated with his love for a woman when his only child, a son, was ten year old, he wrote a number of love poems. In these poems unobtainable women featured. He himself admits:

My poems were born of love, of love's selfishness and of a huge self-pity, like the poems of many whom I admire. And it was only of myself I thought as words took possession of my senses, measured me and linked me with the fabled kingdom of love.[6] (10)

His love poems were brought out in two small volumes, *Close the Sky, Ten by Ten* and *Svayamvara and Other Poems*, both published in 1971. The poems in these two early volumes dealing with the intimacy and passion of love were contrived and abstract in nature, though in them the seeds of his future poetry were already sown. Here were for his favourite images of sun and nun, beggar, helpless women and children.

The responses of these two volumes were mixed. Some of the reviewers were optimistic about the use of images and in the powerful play of imagination. These reviews spoke of "an unquestionable vein of poetry", "a deft, surrealistic arrangement of words," "care and elegance," "lyrical enchanting"(*The Sunday Statesman*), "robust tenderness and gentleness" and "an intensely realised experience" (62). Many other reviews made a scathing attack on the inherent drawbacks in the form and contents of Mahapatra's poetry. Writing love poems, he ran the risk of "fall(ing) into the root of meaningless verbiage"(*The Sunday Statesman*). In order to present this worn-out theme strikingly, he had to experiment with unconventional diction and syntax, and it is precisely on this score that he was mostly faulted. However, commenting on his first two books and conceding to Adil Jussawalla's observation that he was a "Poem-maker," Mahapatra says:

> My first two books of verse were mainly experimental; it was the language again I wanted to exploit, because I felt I would mould it like clay, and I suppose Adil Jussawalla was right in his own way when he said in a review that I was a "poem-maker."[7] (60)

He was, at this stage, desperately trying to come to grips with the medium, with the tools with which he was to build his vision in future work. Thus the two early volumes of Mahapatra's poetry lacked depth and range though they were apparently elegant and lyrical.

There are forty-nine poems in *Close the Sky, Ten by Ten* (1971). They exhibit varying degrees of lyrical qualities: internal assonance and end-rhymes are the common devices used here. There are also grammatical peculiarities, which are typical of Mahapatra, such as omission of some verbs, incomplete lines, and incomprehensible or illogical sentences. Some of the poems in *Close the Sky, Ten by Ten* are cryptic. In "Woman," two parallel statements are juxtaposed without any comment or observation by the poet. They seem trivial and insignificant yet, looked from the other angle, they encourage multiple possibilities:

WOMAN
Even
when she is
Even
when she is not ("Woman", n.p)

The absence of punctuation leaves the clauses open-ended: any termination can be added to it. For example – Even when she is, I feel lonely; unhappy; miserable and so on ("lonely" seems more appropriate because the volume opens with the poem "Loneliness" which is a dominant mood in Mahapatra's poetry throughout) OR – Even when she is not, I live my life; I am not happy; I don't feel lost and so on. Thus the elasticity of the poem expands.

In *A Father's Hours* (1976), Jayanta Mahapatra carries his experimentation a step further by attempting to write longer poems, a forerunner to *Relationship* and *Temple*: "Performance" is a poem with VII sections / 145 lines; "The Twentyfifth Anniversary of a Republic: 1975" with XX sections / 158 lines. A sense of guilt, fear and death looms large in this volume:

> Like a cafe's chair turned over with their legs in the air
>
> perhaps our past lives are raised in surrender to the sky.[8]

The poet is torn between the past and present. His obsession with the past – cultural, social, and individual – makes him a natural outsider in the present. "What is the order of life?" (32) – he asks. How to live meaningfully? The answer perhaps lies in inheriting the past, and in integrating the past to the present, so that the roots do not die and the new branches may imbibe the strengths of a culture that sustained and nourished generations of our ancestors. By discarding that Past as worthless, a romantic's idle dream, a great damage has been done to the quality of our lives. We are now living in a fragmented world, locking ourselves in a cultural vaccum which has resulted in what is traditionally known as *Trishanku Stiti* – neither there nor here: permanently suspended in mid-air upside down.

A Rain of Rites (1976) is Mahapatra's first book of poems published abroad. Though *A Father's Hours* was also published simultaneously in India, after a long gap of five years from his previous volumes, *A Rain of Rites* seems to have matured more during the interval, both thematically and structurally. In "Hunger", Mahapatra portrays with subtle irony the moral degradation of poverty-stricken men and women. The fisherman accepts his young daughter's prostitution and his careless, business-like tone is appaling:

> The fisherman said: will you have her, carelessly, ...
>
> I heard him say: my daughter, she is just turned fifteen . . .
>
> Feel her. I will be back soon, your bus leaves at nine.[9]

Loveless lust is degrading, abhorring and the matter-of-fact narration only intensifies the effect without being emotional, sentimental or sarcastic. Poverty and hunger, the twin-curse of mankind, debase man and women to such low levels that their sensitivity dies and nothing remains sacred or respectable anymore. Human relationships lose all their significance and people merely exist: the struggle for survival consumes a life-time bereft of all hopes! This hunger and deprivation, though a shameful reality for us, appeals readily to the West because it conforms ideally to the expectations of a vast majority of foreign audience that India is a country of beggars, *Sadhus* and snake-charmers.

Waiting (1979) consists of forty-six poems. Mahapatra's self-exploration in the cultural matrix of his social milieu form the dominant theme of this volume. His ruminations over the significance of life and its meaning bind him to Orissa's past, both cultural and historical, which have shaped his personal part. Mahapatra's need to belong to his place that invariably compels him to define all the factors that have contributed to the making of his personality. Infact, Mahapatra's poetry reflects his constant quest at self-definition in "Song of the Past":

> What is real is this
> wistful dreaming about the axis of the past
> and this my body, like a law of gravity,
> held forever, lost in insistent earth and fire.[10]

In *Waiting*, Mahapatra attempts to equate the general and the specific, the remote past and the immediate present, placing himself at the centre of the artistic mediation which defines the aesthetics and the nature of Mahapatra's poetic pursuits. It also reflects a dismal and fearful degeneration of all those human endeavours which are generally considered the hallmarks of any great civilisation. Jayanta Mahapatra responds to these prime concern of human activity and records the dark side of the glory that was. *Waiting* marks the beginning of this shift in Mahapatra's poetry and thus seems justified.

Jayanta Mahapatra's search for meaning, both in life and his relationships with the external world, takes him through a series of encounters between dream and reality in *The False Start* (1980):

There's
a summer hiding away behind the hills,
a haunting dream whose meaning
always escape me,
like the sad shut tufts of mimosa,
hanging there tame and weeping
for the lost touch.[11]

His awareness is conditioned and created by these encounters which are central to his experience. The image of "mimosa" is very aptly used. It is appropriate to the mood. Density of imagery, a common enough device with Mahapatra, is not found here, but one single image taken to its logical conclusion. A simple touch causes the mimosa leaves to shut. Experience and its probable significance are so intricately connected that any attempt to perceive them separately seems ludicrous. That is why the meaning is always elusive, leaving the protagonist to a perpetual tension – a game of hide and seek: the more he seeks the less he perceives, but it is always there like a closely guarded secret. Therefore, *The False Start* contains such poems of Mahapatra's fragmentary experiences which fail to coalesce into a meaningful whole and which often produce a disturbing sense of irritability. But what is comforting is Mahapatra's relentless attempts at portraying the inner conflicts of a man whose constant companions are pain and despair, inadequacy and failure.

Relationship (1980) was published in the same year of the publication of *The False Start*, in its nature and scope, it is remarkably different from all the volumes that preceded it. *Relationship* is the first long poem of "six hundred-plus lines" in twelve sections which is profoundly philosophical and highly contemplative in nature. It dwells in a sustained fashion, on the poet's relationship to his past and those from the past that live on in the lives of the people around him. It uses a raised tone, a heightened diction, longer and more leisurely sentences, and an introductory announcement of the theme in the manner of an epic. This long poem won Mahapatra the Sahitya Akademi Award, the highest honour this country bestows on Literature. It was meant to be an epic, one of the longest poems in Indian writing in English. Mahapatra focuses in this poem on the history, the mythic origin of Orissa. It is, once more, journey of and into the inner life of the poet: sometimes communicated, sometimes mysteriously concealed.

Relationship is representative of the essence of Mahapatra's probing into the eternal questions men have tried to answer generation after generation, i.e., myth of origin, man's place in the Universe, the quality of life, man's role in society and above all, the significance and meaning of existence, man's relationship with himself and the world at large.

> I know I can never come alive
>
> if I refuse to consecrate at the altar of my origins [. . .].[12]

It is an imaginary dialogue with the *self* – what may be termed as Thinking Aloud – which compels the poet to observe, interpret and perhaps understand what is elusive, transcendental and cosmic in nature through the ruins of history, more specifically the history of the land of Orissa and its people. Hence, Mahapatra's *Relationship* is a journey of the awakened conscience back and forth in Time and Space with rich echoes form the silent valleys of the Vedas and the ritualistic Tantrism invoking magic and myth of creation. In *Relationship* linguistic skills have reached a high level of sophistication in their metaphoric mode and opaqueness, as a result of which a highly personal idiom is evolved. Hence, Mahapatra's emphasis on the equally persistent basic human qualities of aggressiveness, sexuality, pain and suffering together create a poetry of enduring quality in *Relationship*.

Life Signs (1983) deals with a medley of questions and problems faced by the poet subjectively and objectively.

In this process he moves slowly but steadily towards what he calls "the centre of your web" (19). This centre is the meeting point of the self and the world. His creation of a personal world – his drive towards the "centre of your web" – is achieved in this period through *Life Signs*, where there is an emphasis on the physical dimension of the external world vis-à-vis his inner feeling. As Bruce King aptly observes, "to bridge as epistemological, phenomenological gap – to know, be part of, enclose experience – with the world and the other, whether it be a woman, temple stones, a Hindu priest" (206).

The signs of life in Mahapatra's world as captured in *Life Signs* include temple priests, solar eclipses, life by the river and sea, devotees and hippies, desolate rice fields, fire flies, ancestors and ruins. The description of these sites and everyday situations, inherited religion and lived life acquire the proportions of vignettes. The sea, the river, water and rain that ran through the expanse of his poetry like veins and arteries now attain new dimensions.

Creativity is always viewed as a superior gift to mankind and surely a poet in the throes of creation is worth observing. The poet as creator is different from the poet as man. How does a poem come into being? Jayanta Mahapatra explains it thus in "Last Night the Poem."

Like the sound of a match striking, then over:
I know that much.[13]

That is, one can only be a witness to that fleeting moment of creative endeavour. You know that it has caught fire, but there is nothing to prolong the experience or better still, the phenomenon is its own interpretations.

The mirror grown so small,

that it doesn't show any image at all (34).

A poem, when completed, has an independent existence of its own, and even its creator the poet, remains an outsider to the experience of the poem, and is compelled to approach it like any other chance reader who may stumble at its threshold. A poem reveals its inner world only to a discerning reader. Its subtle composition demands the utmost patience and care so that a participatory response congenial to the re-enactment of the poet's sequence is created in the reader's mind. Without this reciprocal response, the vehicle of communication becomes impaired.

> Words, brittle like weeds or grass growing under stones,
>
> that break at the slightest touch (34).

True poetry should effectively break the barriers of communication and when Thought becomes Expression, medium is of no significance and the poet loses his personality or his experience becomes that of the readers'. *Life Signs*, is thus of Mahapatra's uneven but eventful poetic path in which the poet and his medium succeeds in sustaining the stubborn stability of being grown up twins. There is a marked growth in their mutual affinity in the common segments of experience, whether it is the area of darkness or the area of dream.

In *Dispossessed Nests: The 1984 Poems*, Jayanta Mahapatra shifted the locale and the centre of his poetry. In *Dispossessed Nests: The 1984 Poems*, the poet attempts to capture the mood of violence in the Punjab and the industrial disaster in Bhopal. The 1984 – poems in this volume mark the poet's shifting of gravity and broadening of his horizon; thematically, the poet goes beyond his province. In that year's violence in the Punjab and the catastrophe of gas-leakage in Bhopal, Mahapatra responded to the mood of the time, condemning the barbaric madness and bringing in God to question: "Must you dry up the river to hear the sands / breathe? Is your hate of man your ultimate fate?" (15). Mahapatra now ponders over the loss of human concern: "to be human / is to see in a dream perhaps / the one who can never be seen" (20). In such a state one is left wonder about "the dispossessed nests" "in the mind's expanding nova" (23).

The poet articulates the suffering of people in the rhetoric of his country's turbulence. Though the images are traditional like riverbed, sea, sky, land, they are seen in the context of a suffering community. Infact, this is the only time when Mahapatra allows himself the luxury or freedom of moving away from the ruins of Orissa – landscape which, otherwise is at the core of all his poetic musings. Here, the subject matter is lucid, real and familiar to the majority of people, and therefore highly readable. For example, the following lines needs no interpretation for their understanding and pose no challenge to the imagination of the reader.

> Around
> a slender waist
> a petticoat stirs
> in the wind,
> looking absurd,
> the torso
> looking about
> for its missing head.
> Pale moonlight
> tills
> death's wild land,
> a coil of smoke
> seems
> to lift its hands
> in supplication[14] (18).

In *Dispossessed Nests: The 1984 Poems,* taken as a whole, Mahapatra tends to rescue his poetry from degenerating to what may be called an instantaneous emotional response to the horrors of human sufferings and violence. Here, Mahapatra seems to have been tempted more by what the future might make of these twin tragedies of human making.

In *Burden of Waves and Fruits* (1988) his dilemma and confrontation with the process of ageing and examined profoundly. This move may said to be the most personal of all he has ever said in his poetry. In this volume, Mahapatra ponders over, in a deeply contemplative mood and reflective tone, what captures his fortile imagination and what burdens his conscience with a heaviness that becomes impossible to bear. A poet is a captive of his thoughts and imagination though he willingly submits himself to their demands. The process of artistic creation is mysterious; it can neither be forced nor can its phase be accelerated.

It is no use trying to put off the instant when it comes, or even taking it by force. Can one tell why various writers have emptied themselves to the cruel caricature which memory dangles as bait before them?

Like a victim it takes advantage of the occasion to deny momentarily the pursuers of their powers.[15]

The whole process has a liberating effect on the poet. Once the poet's "burden" is transformed into a communicable experience through the vehicle of language, the poet experiences a tremendous sense of freedom and relief. *Burden of Waves and Fruits* is Mahapatra's justification of his poetic pursuits which flow from his fountain-spirit so naturally that nothing can stop them or change their course. Hence, Mahapatra's identification with his inner *creative self* is unpretentious and total. This sincerity invests his poetry with an individually all his own. Over the years Mahapatra has matured both as a poet and man, and poetry has become the means of proving to himself that he *IS*.

Jayanta Mahapatra's second long poem *Temple* was published in 1989. It is an attempt to build meaningful bridges with India's present. The poem is a comment on the horror, the social wrongs perpetrated in contemporary times in India, in a half poetic, half dramatic manner. Here, Jayanta Mahapatra, in conceiving the body of a woman as temple and constructing a poem out of it, has made arbitrary inner divisions in *Temple*. Yet, he has kept the main structure of his long poem intact. The structure of *Temple* is in the pattern of the architecture and the spirit of the Orissan temples. These three parts of *Temple* are: "The Hall of Dancing," "The Hall of Offering" and "Sanctum Sanctorum: The Shrine." And, then, there is "the Prologue." This structure is suggestive of the three-fold division corresponds to three broad stages of a woman's life – girlhood, marriage and motherhood. Secondly, the movement from first one section to another denotes the reader's realisation of the ultimate vision where, as the poet puts it, "the real and imagined calmly coalesce," (18).

The Prologue is a newspaper story of an Octogenarian, childless couple belonging to the weaver's community, Ramanujan (85) and Chelammal (80) committing suicide. The poem ends with another news item that speaks of a twelve-year old girl being gangraped and murdered in Khagaria district of the state Orissa. These items suggest the endless sufferings of the Indian woman which is indeed the basic concern of *Temple*. Therefore, the titles seem to indicate Mahapatra's declared theme of *Temple*:

> woman, woman who represents sakti in Hindu mythology – both creator and destroyer.[16] (149).

A Whiteness of Bone was published in 1992. It may be called the compendium of Mahapatra's poetic world because all his major thematic preoccupations find a place in this volume. We see Mahapatra's brooding over what constitutes the essence of his poetic personality. The mood is highly contemplative and deeply introspective. Ineffectiveness, impotency, futility, inaction, death, these are the words and worlds in which Mahapatra traces the origin of his poetry, into the sands of which the ostrich within him buries his head as a defence mechanism. His position is such, his confrontation with a hostile world is to no avail; he knows it yet he cannot ignore it. This complexity informs the art of Jayanta Mahapatra.

In one of the poem dealing with this dilemma is "All the Poetry there Is" in *A Whiteness of Bone*. In this poem Mahapatra's stand on the role of a poet is clearly pronounced. It begins dramatically with "All the poetry there is in the world / appears to rise out of the ashes" that echoes the Biblical wisdom: "Dust thou art, and unto dust shalt thou return." The world it goes on to create is a quiet and sombre one where one is humbled as one comes to know its cruelties. In a world like this "twenty persons were gunned down" for no fault of theirs. He cannot re-structure the world out there. He builds a world of his own, in his poetry consoling himself:

> Poetry simply wants to know what sort of thing
>
> war was, or a sunset, even a bizarre crime.[17](9)
>
> If this can be the way with poetry, it "doesn't have to raise its voice."(9)

How ostrich-like the poet is! However hostile, like a desert, his world might be, he cannot live elsewhere. He will live in the world yet bury his head in the act of writing poetry. It is through this paradox that he hopes to alleviate his pain and agony. For this the poet needs to have an inner-detachment. Earlier, Mahapatra used to be pure, uncontaminated inner world, the socio-cultural and mythic details of the past and the pastness of the present economic and political world. Now, he constructs his poetic world on the bad news of the present rather than on the golden past. *A Whiteness of Bone* is a collection of such poems that creates a catalogue of catastrophes that have ripped India into shreds, emotionally. Some of them are violence, mindless bloodshed in the province of the Punjab, thousands dead due to gas-leakage in the Union Carbide factory at Bhopal, assassination of Indira Gandhi, Delhi riots and the self-immolation by fire of students protesting against the implementation of caste law recommended by Mondal Commission. Therefore, according to Mahapatra, the task of transforming the society has to begin from reforming the minds of the individuals. Such a change then, is most likely to be in the desired direction, as it is born of pain and suffering, which has the ability to redeem the sufferer.

The Best of Jayanta Mahapatra is a selection of best poems of Mahapatra published in 1995 from his book *A Rain of Rites* (1976) to *A Whiteness of Bone* (1992) and an autobiographical prose-fragment, edited by P.P. Raveendran, is considered to be the best representative selected work of Jayanta Mahapatra. In his introductory note, Raveendran highlights Mahapatra's act of decolonising Indian English Poetry: "Alone of all Indian poets writing with the possible exception of A.K. Ramanujan, it is in Jayanta Mahapatra's poetry, that this decolonising act takes on a quality and specificity comparable to the best verse written in Indian regional languages"[18] (13). Mahapatra has also succeeded in "decolonising the self by confronting the colonial ideology. The first goal he achieves, is by concerning himself more and more with history, both racial and personal" (191-193).

His prose autobiographical fragment is poetic which sketches some moments of his childhood days. Entitled as 'The Door', it reflects the image of 'Door' in his poetry, through which he has been to look out into the world – the inner and outer. In the concluding line, he asserts that solemnly: "But I cannot purge myself of that jungle, of that wasteland, where a bit of my childhood knocks still on that dark-faced door in stubborn silence" (152).

In Jayanta Mahapatra's *Shadow Space* (1997) poems are often referred to as counter-measures to overcome the feeling of guilt, of impotency at not being able to do anything corrective or constructive with his poems when the world is not as it should be:

> Indefinable, like life, with the government wrong,
> the thinking wrong, the world wrong.
> But the irony is beautiful [. . .].[19] (49)

The variation of the reference to poetry, his own or poetry as a genre, questioning its efficacy in *Shadow Space*. The poems in this volume very obviously step out on to the street and into the remote village, in order to express the poet's anguish about contemporary society. The inexplicable and ruthless violence and injustice of contemporary society has begun to worry the poet. The first poem in *Shadow Space* 'Living in Orissa' speaks of the shadow of the past, a 'fatal spirit' that refuses to go:

> Something here, perhaps fatal spirit.
> Something that recalls the centuries of defeat.
> [. . .].
> Today the darkness of our own shadows
> slips over the uncared-for cemeteries by the river.
> [. . .].
> Only shadows shift now.
> They have the eyes of defeated spirits.
> The old old eyes.[19] (11)

The concept of the past in this poem differs from the earlier works. The past here is the spirit unable to change – dead customs, 'uncomprehended totems' – that do not transform towards health and light that remain 'antlered in sickness and disease' referring to the appaling conditions prevailing amongst the tribals and other marginalised sections of society in Orissa, and of course, the rest of the country. Hence, a large number of poems in this volume deals with contemporary social issues with a nervous energy that succeeds in creating good poetry.

With the publication of *Bare Face* in the year 2000 which is certainly termed as a literary epoch. This elegantly produced collection has simply reaffirmed his position as a most flourishing Indian English Poet. Of late Mahapatra's poetry has started assuming some what political overtones but his richly textured voice still broods meditatively over centuries of decay and sufferings, a sense of disillusionment, sufferings of women – a logical extension of his world with recurring and evocative images of night, shadow, rain, darkness, light, death:

> Rain, all night.
>
> Capacious, like the body of a woman.
>
> [. . .].
>
> The saints are all silent inside their own truths.
>
> Moss broods silently in the cracks of the stone.
>
> [. . .].
>
> And this evening, too, silent as yesterday
>
> swaying on its darkness inside the arithmetic of rain.[20]
> (13)

For Mahapatra, every poem reflects an existential dilemma. The dilemma of having to face the day square on its face with all its uncertainties, his helplessness to alter the charted course of history, the inevitability he cannot escape, his supple imagination resonant with a subtle irony:

> Today, no one I know has died in our street;
> when I go out I will meet the same people again
> and act with the same polite formality
> as we did when they first spoke to me;
> the carefully kept distance between us
> starts shaking its head.[20] (40)

Nothing, infact, has changed and yet it has been phenomenal, for poem after poem we came across yet another face of Jayanta Mahapatra who has traversed the rugged landscape to just flat, lucid statements of poetry and one who has the acute inward tone of his poetry for all the externalities of the word. For someone who has always been branded as 'difficult' or 'obscure' the poetic journey has been a virtual turnaround. Almost all the poems in *Bare Face* stand testimony to this.

Mahapatra's latest volume *Random Descent* was published in the year 2005 picks up some modes of his thoughts randomly. A serious thinker of the sorrows of the downtrodden and the women-class at large, Mahapatra is still profoundly meditative, with a tragic vision of life and the fate of his land over the centuries till todate. Divided into three sections, this collection of poetry is a fresh recurrence of the old legends, the poet was elaborating through out the past three decades.

In the first section titled "Old Violins of Legends" there are thirty-five poems which reminds us of Mahapatra's constant proneness to grief, sorrow, silence, pain and darkness. Here there is the loss of hope, and there the pain stands atrocious and tyrannical. The poet's mother, winter in his city, siberian geese in the lake of chilka, his grandfather embracing christianity at his sixteen out of acute starvation, the lost Kalinga war, a brief winter in Orissa and the stone which stand for the centrality of Orissa's architectural cosmogony and several other old concerns assume shapes of profound thought. He is very much disturbed about the social turmoils of the present era. Killings of innocent people every-where in the world, widespread terrorism and insurgency disturb him. Out of deep sorrow he speaks out:

Today I don't know whether
God wants to be a part of my life.
How does one know what is real any more?
Senseless killings hold up their hands to silence me.[21]
(22)

The sorry picture of the surroundings has been his constant obsession. The persistent degeneration and gloominess asphyxiate the poet's soul. He picks up a few images to depict the pervasive darkness and sorrow:

Somewhere, inside a room,
a girl is dying in her mother's arms.
Elsewhere, someone

revenges himself for his broken life.
I look at people. At my little misery.[21] (21)

Mahapatra's favourite images of 'stone' assume new dimensions of meaning in his recent poetry. The 'stone' through the years has been changed. As such the poet utters:

I have no choice today
The house I have lived in all these years
has forgotten the stone it was made of

Beneath the bloodied walls of history
nothing can happen more dreadful
than stones turned to gods through prayers
Stones, whose eyes have had no expression in them
Stones, like governments, who have no honour at all
Stones, whose long arms easily batter and kill
a young woman accused of adultery[21] (47)

The poet's socialist ideology is still an obsession with him. His failure at achieving the desired fulfilment of the social upliftment has made him frustrated and mute all along. He now feels his existence to be a 'shadow' and he is only dangling in a 'shadow space', living in his puppet land, not the promised land. 'The promised land' is a land of peace and prosperity and social equity which in Gandhiji's vision was the 'Ramrajya.' So the aggrieved poet bewails:

These days
I move into the shadow of myself,
not trying to understand
the words other try to weigh me with.
I accept what I see through the open window
and between its rigid iron bars,
not the Man who for years
desired a country in vain and then
fell in love with the first puppet land they gave him,
even if it failed
to correspond exactly with the promised land.[21] (54-55)

The second section titled "Another Ruined Country, 2002" contains ten poems depicting some ruins of the year 2002. The persistent tragic vision rolls before the poet's mind's eyes. A raped sixteen year old girl, blind alleys of the city, a little girl's raped body, cries of women made hostages, a never ending scream of suffering and hatred, long speeches of the politicians, an orphan girl, a maimed man, and a ruined country are the several subjects of these poems. The poet strongly says that this ruined land is not the land of his vision. He does not want to live in this land. He says:

The land some love to call holy
is not the one I want to live in.
Today the land of shrines and temples
offers its troubled tombs of blood,
when I don't want to write my poem,
while a mob watches, cheering in delight
at the sight of Fara's rape
and mutilation limb by limb.[21] (70)

Thus the poet bravely declares his desires:

I want the graveyard to flower without its corpses,
and the sunlit street
to shine without its shadows.
I want the flames to warm the empty heart
of love, not burn a city with pitiable hatred.
I don't want to sit bent over a page
to reflect in it my griefs,
more for myself than for others.
I want my government to hover
like a butterfly over a garden;
not be, as it is, like a wasp or snake.[21] (70)

Now Mahapatra's poetry of non-comment turns to be

the poetry of comment. It is the poetry voicing his protest and intolerance against the sufferings of the poor, weak and down trodden of the land. He wants to safeguard the poor sufferer and become their saviour. He further exposes his intention:

> I only want to renew myself
> like this old river's quiet
> that has emerged victorious
> over a hundred layers of religion
> in the airlessness of the dead.[21] (70)

The third and final section titled "Shores of Darkness and Light" contains four poems. In this section, the poet's favourite images of 'darkness' and 'light' emerge with renewed possibilities. Amidst the darkness and light, the persona is tossed, twisted and tamed. He is compelled to accept the turnouts of the time. Thus in his confession of the sad state of existence, he presents a poetry of humility:

> Something in the light withers me into a shadow
> of myself. I begin to make foolish demands
> to ward off the fine rain of fear.
> This time is a fish out of water.
> And our bodies bear the old marks of its thrashings.[21]
> (74)

Taken as a whole, Jayanta Mahapatra's poetry demonstrates the gradual evolution of the poet from the stages of his unsteady grouping in the dark to the level of finding a personal voice. What needs to be appreciated are Mahapatra's persistent efforts to explore the dark recesses of the human soul which act as a constraint for self actualisation. All his poetry, therefore is a journey into the *self* in an attempt to understand the mysteries of life. Mahapatra affirms:

> My poetry has always been one of questioning, of trying to find answer, of being on the border between the known and unknown, around the mysterious.[22]

REFERENCES

1. Quoted by Paul C. Verghese, *Problems of the Indian Creative Writer in English*. Bombay: Somaiya Publication Private Ltd., 1971. 179.
2. Parthasarthy, R., ed. *Ten Twentieth Century Indian Poets*. New Delhi: Oxford University Press 1986.
3. Narasimhaiah, C.D. *The Swan and the Eagle*. Shimla: Indian Institute of Advanced Study, 1969. 29.
4. Mahapatra, Jayanta., "Even If No One takes My Poems Seriously" *Chandrabhaga* 4 Winter 1980. 69.
5. Raghavan, N. "Inner View: N. Raghavan talks to Jayanta Mahapatra," *Tenor*, No.1 1978. 59.
6. Mahapatra, Jayanta., "The Poet's Blues," *Youth Times*, VII, 17, Bombay: 1980. 10-11.
7. Raghavan, N. "Inner View: N. Raghavan talks to Jayanta Mahapatra," *Tenor*, No.1 1978. 60.
8. Mahapatra, Jayanta., "The Twentyfifth Anniversary of a Republic: 1975," *A Father's Hours*. Calcutta: United Writers, 1976. 32.
9. Mahapatra, Jayanta., "Hunger," *A Rain of Rites*. Athens: The University of Georgia Press, 1976. 44.
10. Mahapatra, Jayanta., *Waiting*. New Delhi: Samkaleen Prakashan, 1979. 13.
11. Mahapatra, Jayanta. *The False Start*. Bombay: Clearing House, 1980. 13.
12. Mahapatra, Jayanta. *Relationship*. New York: The Greenfield Review Press, 1980. 18.
13. Mahapatra, Jayanta., "Last Night The Poem," *Life Signs*. New Delhi: Oxford University Press, 1983. 34.
14. Mahapatra, Jayanta. *Dispossessed Nests: The 1984 Poems*. Jaipur: Nirala Publications, 1986. 18.
15. Mahapatra, Jayanta. *Burden of Waves and Fruits: Poems*. Washington, D.C.: Three Continents Press, 1988.
16. Mahapatra, Jayanta. *Autobiography: Contemporary Author's Autobiographical Series*. 149.
17. Mahapatra, Jayanta. *A Whiteness of Bone*. New Delhi: Viking, Penguin Books India Private Ltd. 1992. 09.

18. Mahapatra, Jayanta. *The Best of Jayanta Mahapatra*. Kozikode: Bodhi Publishers, 1995. 13.
19. Mahapatra, Jayanta. *Shadow Space*. Kottayam: DC Books, 1997. 49,11.
20. Mahapatra. Jayanta. *Bare Face*. Kottayam: DC Books, 2001. 13,40.
21. Mahapatra,Jayanta. *Random Descent*. Bhubaneshwar:Third Eye Communications, 2005. 21-22,47,54-55,70,74.
22. Mahapatra, Jayanta., Interview by Aruna Ludra. *The Indian Literary Review* 7. 1-3 Jan, Apr, Oct. 1991: 53.

2

His Philosophical Humanism

This chapter intends to record Jayanta Mahapatra as a humanist in the trinity of "religion", "culture" and "time." His 'religion' is a belief in humanistic values; his 'culture' represents refinement of those values; and time-consciousness signifies the complexity of experiences of life and also the present as an interminable extension of the past into future, which is deeply rooted in the past. And words are too inadequate for the poet to express his feelings, and therefore Mahapatra has learnt "to talk with his heart." And only when a poet talks with his heart about an experience of life, an idea about that experience gels into a perfect poetic art in his mind. And the poet becomes the poetry, and the poetry, in turn, tends to become the reader or the critic. And the poet, the poetry and the reader are all fused into a 'whole' or 'Absolute'.

Mahapatra's poetry manifests his struggle with word-structures to create a meaning. Often a thought or an image or a mood starts him on his poetic voyage. He is led blindfold into a whirlpool of disturbing and recalcitrant realities in search of significance and meaning. The quest for appropriate alternatives – to transform his suffering and pain into pregnant images and metaphors – forms the nucleus of Mahapatra's constant pursuit. The nature of this exploration is a mystery even to him also:

My poems remain exploratory, because when I am heading to; the first image merely starts a *movement* of a poem. It is as if I am at the entrance of a cave and I have to proceed, not knowing where the exploratory path leads me.[1]

"The Indian Eye" from *Close the Sky, Ten by Ten* offers an insight to this problems of Mahapatra's poetic mediation. In order to understand the poem, we need to look into the socio-religious background of giving alms to the needy and deserving which is considered a sacred duty. Beggary exists in India in many levels and forms. No doubt it is mostly a social evil, but we cannot turn a blind eye to the fact that beggary has its sanctions in religious beliefs and practices too. Legend has it that even Lord Shiva had to go begging in retribution for having plucked one of the five faces of Lord Bramha. Ascetics and *Sadhus* live on charity: the begging-bowl is an inseparable part of their lives. At the same time, we must not forget that beggary has been turned into an easy and profitable profession now by inherently indolent people. In olden days it was not uncommon for the students after having completed their studies in the *Gurukulas*, to approach the affluent merchants or kings for help to pay off their gurudakshina and if the donor, for whatever reasons, was not in a position to render help, felt miserable. Mahapatra is perhaps alluding to this age-old tradition, when he writes, "if you part with a coin, you'd reap a solid million." But what the poet now observes in the contemporary society in "The Indian Eye" is far from being noble:

> Looking, eyes shut, for fear of contamination,
> When I step out of the door, The Indian eye
> Is large, wild, covered with hungry decomposition.
>
> Years and years lay claim to safe paralytic tradition.
> Turning sharply as if to avoid a muddy puddle,
> While their begging hands are at you, sacred god like
> you.
> Now if you part with a coin, you'd reap a solid million.
> You are god, they cry, tear your eyes from you,
> And if you are not you turn to the wall and cry.

(*Close the Sky, Ten by Ten,* n.p)

The poet's sympathies and his impotent rage tear him apart. Now, beggary is degraded under the cover of a "safe paralytic tradition". The tradition has now become paralytic losing its once religiously sanctioned function, whereby the society supported the intellectuals and the holy men. Ironically, it also represents the plight of beggars, who are dependent on charity and live like parasites. Even the donors have lost their nobility of heart and soul. Hence, charity is practiced often to cover up the illegal means employed in amassing wealth and gaining popularity. A corruption of tastes and commercialization of cultures is what "The Indian Eye" registers. If we look with our eyes wide open there is always a "fear of contamination". If we shut our eyes, we begin to introspect, see within ourselves, and perhaps realise that the "large, wild Indian eye is covered with hungry decomposition". What we see as social realities are nothing but an external manifestation of this very degradation; and what is worse, the very sources – tradition and culture – from which to draw inspiration are dried up beyond redemption. However, the alternative may be to "turn to the wall and cry", hopefully perhaps, for a revival and rejuvenation of our vital energies to sustain our moral rectitude. If this is not to be,

tomorrow will find him
where he is now. Putting
his darkness on the line ·
("The Blind Beggar", *Close the Sky, Ten by Ten,* n.p)

Jayanta Mahapatra invests his symbols with multiple meanings by compressing the images even when he deals with a concrete situation like for example, a beggar in a train, which is a common enough sight in any part of India. The miserable plight of a blind beggar in a "guzzling train" is depicted in the poem titled "Blind Singer in a Train", through a series of densely textured images, which reinforce his tragic situation without the slightest melodramatic element:

> Between successive halts of the guzzling train,
> this bamboo-stabled man, rooted
> to his night, flutters stone wings as he faces
> the clash of silver, the prim dawn-light
> rushing past his pox-hollowed eyes (33).

The image used here clearly indicate a sense of helpless entrapment forever, which constitutes tragic irony of man's destiny in a cruel and unkind world. First of all, the man is blind – a physical handicap for which he is not responsible. Loss of vision has confined him to night and without his bamboo stick he cannot move about. Hence, he is "rooted to his night" like a tree, with no hopes of ever moving away from the engulfing darkness. A blind man's constant support is his bamboo-stick and he comes to increasingly depend on it. Jayanta Mahapatra coins a new compound word "bamboo-stabled man", which suggests that the blind man gains stability by his stick, and his plight is no better than an animal tethered to a pole in a stable. The animal's well-being depends on the nature of its master whether he is kind or not. A beggar is doubly handicapped because he is at the mercy of his fellow-men and the philanthropic, the generous and kind-hearted are not found everywhere. He has to try to locate a kind soul amidst a thousand hostile faces "who turn (their) cultured heads away" at the sight of an appropriate beggar. This is an example of compression of images, which is Jayanta Mahapatra's favourite technique. This image is taken up in the second stanza where "the faded stick's tap of hope" is faintly heard in a moving train which is a "packed box". It is not the hope that is faded but the very stick that supports the blind man is "faded". Then how can there be a better tomorrow for the millions of those who are condemned to permanent drudgery and dependency for no fault of their own? The "prim dawn-light" rushes past them as they have only terrible looking hollows for eyes- a gift of small pox! Light and all that it represents is forever stolen from them, so also their future, as their "pox-hollowed eyes" stare blindly into a vacant tomorrow:

> The academic ones walk to his calculated steps
> across the packed box, hear the faded stick's
> tap of hope in the daily functions of spider-
> flesh. Together they induce a spirited caste
> amidst the companions of progression.
>
> Then the ponderous song evokes. To turn
> cultured heads away is the standard
> procedure of the undamaged, who can only hear
> the bones' blind beggary and feel the embarrassed
> contraction of superfluous substance (33).

"Cultured heads" – loquacious academicians or grandiloquent politicians who hold heated discussions on all aspects concerning human civilisation – form only "a spirited caste" and turn their heads away when confronted with a real problem, because they have never experienced the trauma of living a dreadful and a hopeless life. They are "undamaged"! Thus, a blind-beggar's burden of despair that lasts a life time, remains outside the experience of "cultured heads", who are expected to guide and shape the destiny of the nation. The dynamics of social behaviour thus get reflected in Jayanta Mahapatra's poetry, that without being explicit, it points a finger towards the self, making him answer the most vital question: *Am I not partly to blame for all this*? Incidentally, this question also stares the reader in the face demanding an honest answer from him. Jayanta Mahapatra's poetry leaves the matter at that without ever giving his answers or solutions. Thus, Mahapatra avoids the dangers of a propagandistic approach saving his poetry from the pitfalls of a sloganistic reduction by oversimplification. This seems to be the most significant characteristic of Mahapatra's poetry in general.

Jayanta Mahapatra's kaleidoscopic mind forms bright patterns and every time the kaleidoscope is turned new patterns emerge with new shades of meaning. Hence, one should look more into the patterns than their meanings because meanings seem more elusive. For example, the following lines appear in the poem "Sun Worshipper".

> To volatilise matter
>
> in trivial unmeaning (24).

In his best poems, there is an equilibrium established between the two, i.e., meaning and patterns. Mahapatra is breathlessly engrossed in creating his word-order wherein the unwanted shades of meaning are silenced, and then resurrected in a new situation by their strange collocation. Man has been worshiping the Life-giving-Principle of Nature as a token of his gratitude and respect. Sun is the giver of life. In the Vedas there are many hymns in praise of the sun-god. Thus, sun-worship is indeed a celebration of Life-giving-Principle. The poem "Sun Worshipper" illustrates this point:

> With ease he pulls off a silver
> of orange sun in two necessary hands,
> cups them over his head, together.
> The water runs down in vertical lines.
> The dawn suddenly is normal again,
> Life's pattern falls on the gravity
> of the flesh, in a now-stilled posture,
> remote in the harvest of survival (24).

Oblation to the sun is done by taking water in the cup of joined hands, then lifting them up over one's head and powering down the water as from a stream, while chanting *mantras* in praise of the Sun-god for the "harvest of survival" one has received in abundance!

> The lips of the static body pursue
>
> fevered praise while the supersolvent runs,
>
> intensely aware of the abundant green dawning (24).

i.e., when a man prepares to pour oblations, the "orange

sun" is reflected in the water of his cupped hands, looking almost a captive and the down appears to shy away in the tiny hands that hold the mighty Sun. But as soon as "the water runs down", symbolic consummation of *Prakriti* and *Purusha* is achieved. The mighty Sun is then back in his grand chariot drawn by seven horses (symbolising seven days of a week) and everything is bright once again – "The dawn suddenly is normal again". This magical transformation, though a creation of the poet's imagination, is nonetheless vivid and charming. The use of scientific term – "supersolvent" for water – has a special significance: the Life-giving-Principle is held in high reverence through oblations to Sun-god using equally life-sustaining Water-Principle by a deft use of the adjective as noun. Thus, the complementary role of the Earth and the Sky, Prakriti and Purusha, is revered hoping for their fruitful union. This suggestion is further reinforced by "the static body" of the worshipper in a state of full concentration: "static" is not a state of immobility but of deep contemplation, which results in "fevered praise", suggesting a state of high excitement and exaltation of body, mind and spirit in unison. Here, the pathological connotation of the word "fever" is silenced to echo exactly the opposite – a state of vibrant exaltation.

In Mahapatra, a deeply felt personal experience is often internalised creating what Bruce King calls a "poetry of introversion".[2] The experience sinks deep into the layers of sub-conscious, and operates in subtle ways, surfacing unexpectedly in disguised forms. Left alone, a reader has to grope through such Phantom figures. The following lines may be considered as an example to illustrate the point under consideration:

> He stops under a tree, no father, about to die.
> The tree's tight nearness, which has not moved.
> One summer I remember, when we could yes,
> stand together: the fierce crimson crest, his fire,
> that would push, push to tear among the sad

pleasing masks I wore. Do I have answers when
there are no questions, no roots to water anymore?
My father, there is not much time left I know,
as you fall to air; we would not know how those
hurts inside shaped the embrace we'd find tomorrow
("To My Father", *Close the Sky, Ten by Ten*, n.p).

Here, the fading away of life, though sad in itself, is acknowledged as a natural event of the cycle of births and deaths. But the self-preserving instinct of man guides him to "embrace" so that "tomorrow" is born with a new, fresh face and life would go on. The fear of death and the joy of birth succeed each other. We may recall here that in Sanskrit a son is called *atmaja*, i.e., 'I am reborn in my son'. (Cf:"You're quietly pregnant awaiting my birth". "The Builders". *Close the Sky, Ten by Ten*, n.p). The term *atmaja* significantly conveys how the fear of death is reassuringly converted into the solace that one continues to live in his children and in that sense conquers death!

The anticipated fear of something unknown and unnamed has always been with Mahapatra, making his poetry look sinister! It may well be his own sense of incompetence, weakness and incompleteness that keeps haunting him. His poetry is more of a dialogue with the *self*. Hence, a reader has to reconstruct a tangible sequence out of the broken bits he chances to overhear, as it were:

I close my eyes, stretch
the body to stratagem, the to
-and-fro steps pity me;
My thin shadow is identity.
Always, all dreams
breed contempt. How
can i let go, reappear
another time, elsewhere?...
Something i do not wish
to see rests by my side,
touching me, trying

to find my tenderness ("Day Thought". *Close the Sky, Ten by Ten*, n.p).

What marks Mahapatra's poetry as special is the poet's honesty and a serious concern for his craft. He seems to constantly reexamine and re-assess his writings as no other poet perhaps does. For example, Mahapatra confesses:

When I reread the poetry I have written, I find many of the poems confused, made up of abstractions which fail to connect with the reader. This is especially true of my earlier work.[3]

Therefore, Mahapatra's poetry is addressed to a discriminating reader – a *sahrudaya* – who is willing to take pains to encounter the experience held captive within the structure of the poem. The readers' own experience should guide them to unravel the mysteries of Mahapatra's poetic creation. Thus, in Mahapatra we see a generous invitation for reader involvement in the experience of the poem and its re-construction.

In Mahapatra's poetry, the primacy of reader-response is as much valid as the primacy of the text itself. Mahapatra's poetry does not give any message to its readers in the form of a well-phrased witticism. Instead, it makes the reader look inwards, question himself about life, its significance, uncertainty and so on leading him into a process of personal discovery. This indeed is the greatest strength of Mahapatra's poetry.

Jayanta Mahapatra's poetry flows like the calm, majestic Ganga through the vast expanse of the plains. There is no "spontaneous overflow of powerful emotions" but it reflects "emotions recollected in tranquility"(Wordsworth). The poet's role is of a dispassionate, detached observer. In other words, the whole mass of "language material" of Mahapatra's poetry is inseparable from the thought content. That is to say, the mode of linguistic expression itself becomes the commentary of Mahapatra's poetry. Hence, the "language material" by its very organisation aids the reader in introspecting the poetry of Mahapatra.

Mahapatra's poetry sees beyond the superficial existence, in order to sustain the eternal quest of man to understand the *self* has been a recurrent theme in his poetry throughout. Moreover, his poetry makes every attempt to achieve cohesion in the expression of the transcendental and elusive experience through concrete, visual images with multiple suggestiveness as in "The Moon Moments":

> Why does one room invariably lead into other rooms?
> ...
> What humility is that which will not let me reveal
> What shameful secret lies hidden in the shadows of
> my
> moon? (50)

Mahapatra's poetry is an attempt at retrieval-going back to the origin, travelling backwards in time, tracing the footprints of tradition – to discern the meaning of existence.

> the clock jerks each memory towards the present,
>
> to become a past (51).

This retrieval is not a retrogression, but a necessary precondition to advance from the current stage of involuntary stagnation, which results from an ignorance of one's origin, wherein lie the roots of one's existence. Therefore, this backward journey is also an exploration, a meaningful discovery, which promotes our awareness and sensibility. Rabindra K. Swain endorses this view in the following remarks:

> This 'retrieve' of the past as Heidegger calls it is not a nostalgic return but a presenting that uncovers lost possibilities, a going back to go forward.[4]

The co-existence of Life and Death, Absurdity and

Meaningfulness, Good and Evil – a pair of opposite – bears a tremendous significance for the poet because one has meaning only in relation to the other. Mahapatra justifies this pairing of opposites as the reality of this Universe:

> a sense of perfect whole is experienced through a synthesis of opposites: through thought and action, cause and effect through the androgynous principle of ardhanarishwar (half man, half woman).[5]

Our religious symbols offer conclusive evidence to the manifestation of this duality in Nature: for example, goddess Durga is worshipped in her dual role of Creator and Destroyer; man-woman relationship is a classic example of the duality in Nature which is complementary and when segregated, each is incomplete and unfulfilled, but together, they create the world. Similarly, *Vak* (Speech) and *Artha* (Meaning) should merge with each other for total communication, hence the noted Sanskrit poet Kalidasa invokes the blessings of Lord Shiva and Parvati – the Parent of this Universe – in *Kumarasambhava* to grant him the power to create his muse where *Vak* and *Artha* become inseparable: *Vagartha prathipathaye / Jagathaha pitharam vande Parvathee- parameshwaraw* ('For the fusion of Speech and Meaning, Salutations to the Parents of the Universe').

> Mahapatra's poetry is profoundly *philosophical* and highly contemplative in nature. In *Gita,* Krishna says:
>
> Maya thathamidam sarvam jagadavyaktamurtina
>
> Mathsani sarvabhutani na chaham theshwavasthithaha (IX: 4).
>
> ('Everything originates from Me and in Me everything ends. I create all but I am in none'.)

This paradox continues to dominate the conscience of the poet. Mahapatra is painfully aware of the co-existence of paradoxes which he tries to depict. Just as a magnet has south and north poles at the extreme ends of the same magnetic bar pointing to opposite directions, yet inseparably united in a strange way, Mahapatra's poetry communicates the pulls of unresolved opposites. From concrete to the abstract, from the ruins of history – the temples of Konarka – to the glorious past, his probing spirit wanders lonely with a singleness of purpose – the Meaning that would lead to self-realisation: The following lines from William Blake ("Auguries of Innocence") aptly summarise Mahapatra's preoccupations:

> To see a world in a grain of sand and [. . .].
> Hold Infinity in the palm of your hand.

Mahapatra uses certain images and symbols in his poetry like *death, darkness, past, silence, door, etc.,* which become the recurrent motifs of his poetry. Mahapatra's poetry volumes are held in closer relationship by the recurrence of these motifs, as well as by their thematic repetitiveness, which give unity and significance to Mahapatra's modes of perceiving an experience rooted either in the reality of the external world or the interior landscape of his poetic imagination. Mahapatra's poetry is an attempt to relate himself to his environment, to the socio-cultural milieu of his land – Orissa and its history, both ancient and modern. His poetry defines his ways of belonging to what is contemporary in society and what is permanent and elusive in the eternal flux of time.

Death is a recurring, dominant theme in Mahapatra's poetic world. The treatment of death deserves our close attention because it is unconventional in the sense that the poet neither celebrates death nor abhors it as something to be dreaded. Though fear of death manifests on certain occasions, it is never treated as anti-life or even as a means of escape from the dreariness of life. Death gives meaning to life, because in the absence of it, the beauty of life would not be felt.

DEATH → Meaning of Life embedded ← LIFE

The significance of Life is sandwiched between Life and Death. Fear of death guides one back to life, to live more vigorously and more meaningfully. In "Measuring Death", Mahapatra asks,

> But father, isn't it death again
>
> that brought you your meanings of life
>
> and then guided you back to it? (75)

All the same, Life is a steady march towards the inescapable Deaths.

> Death is a handcraft you push,
>
> Through a dayful of moonlight of sadness you can't trust (78).

This is a very striking metaphor. Moonlight is invisible during day time, yet it exists. Similarly death, until it manifests, is there continually about us, a reality to be acknowledged even before it is experientially felt. Death and Life are not two different unrelated abstractions. They are not only complementary but one has significance only in relation to the other; and together they complete the cyclical process in Nature. Mahapatra is aware of being a link in the endless flow of time and Cycle of Births and Deaths. Hence, "burning grounds" are "a place of sacrifice" (4). Death is not the ultimate end. It is the beginning of a new cycle of life.

> The evening fosters light,
>
> and kneeling villages inhabit the beginnings
>
> of a tale that never appears to end (4).

Here, Mahapatra seems to echo the dictum of Shankaracharya.

Punarapi jananam, punarapi maranam
Punarapi jananee jattare shayanam

('To be born again and again, to die again and again and to lay in mother's womb again and again., i.e., until *Nirvana* = *Moksha* / Salvation is attained').

Man has been eternally puzzled by death, and a strong desire to gain power over it is manifest in his quest for permanence, either through religious practices or the Arts or even the Sciences – the three major areas of man's probing. Of course, recourse to religion gives him the necessary impetus since it belongs to the realm of the Metaphysical, which transcends the barriers of Time, Space and sometimes even Logic. It is strongly believed that the pull of the *earth* binds Man to the cycle of birth and death. Gita stresses the complexity of the web of birth and death, in a greater sense, as the Law of Universe, which is binding on everything save – *Brahman* – the Absolute.

Jathasya hi dhruvo mruthyurdhruvam janma mruthasya cha
Thasmadapariharyerthe na tvan: shochitumarhasi (II: 27).
(i.e., 'He who is born shall die and he who dies shall be born again. Therefore, O Arjuna, don't grieve over this unresolvable issue.')
In order to conquer death, man must free himself from the pulls of earth. As Mahapatra puts it,
The waves along the shore
Are fighting away to get free of earth and death
("Absences", *The False Start,* p.16).

Therefore, as per above mentioned lines the poet conveys the eternal nature of such a pursuit by the image of "waves" – waves after waves come and beat against the shore, recede only to come back again, and relentlessly the process is repeated as if there is no end to it. Also, *earth* and *death* are inseparable linked. If man wants to break away from the chain of Births and Deaths he has to free himself from all things that bind him to the earth. Again in the *Gita,* Krishna tells Arjuna that wise men free themselves from the bondage Births by giving up the fruits of their action = Karma (which infact binds them to the earth).

> Karmajam buddhiyukta hi phalam tyaktva maneeshinaha
>
> Janmabandhavinirmuktaha padam gachhantyanamayam (II: 51).

But, we must note that Mahapatra is not advocating spiritual salvation by denouncing this world; instead, by the deft use of the image of waves as explained earlier, he only stresses the near impossibility of such an attempt to rid oneself of the clutches of death. Moreover, the reality is that death gives meaning to life. In "Absences", Mahapatra conveys that in the absence of death, we would not be in a position to perceive this phenomenal world as we do now:

> If there were no death here,
> The common-looking clouds would have blinded our eyes (16).
> Even the common things would be bereft of their beauty and significance and may look grotesque if death did not exist. Alan Kennedy observes:
> Death therefore is the mother of the possibilities of life,
> as it is the mother of desire, making us reach down the dawns for the blinding possibilities of deathless clouds.[6]

This duality inherent in man is one of Mahapatra's major concern. However, his probing into the mystery of death as an inevitable, unavoidable and inescapable end of life and all that life represents, become more significant when compared to his contemporaries like Keki N. Daruwalla, Deba Patnaik and A.K. Ramanujan. Infact, *Death* is a major theme in contemporary Indian poetry in English in general.

Keki N. Daruwalla's attitude to death is in striking contrast to Mahapatra's. Daruwalla accepts that death as a natural process.

> Death hums over the wires [. . .].
> Throughout life a man carries his death
> even as a woman carries her child.[7]

Though a sense of imminent death is there, it fails to illuminate any further as it does in Mahapatra by its metaphysical and philosophical overtures. Daruwalla's depiction of death has the serenity of calm acceptance as an inevitable natural order of events, whereas Mahapatra's treatment of death gains in intensity and depth by its rich suggestiveness as a cyclical process with the much desired regenerative powers.

Deba Patnaik, an expatriate Oriya poet who lives in America, successfully in- corporates philosophical overtones comparable to Mahapatra's whose poetic world is dominated by waiting, brooding silence and loneliness.

> Death is not dying, waiting
> is. [. . .].
> who says death is lonely? Living
> is.[8]

The world of Mahapatra seems to be dominated by "unrelieved darkness, shadows and inertia", where "light" comes painfully without brightening the atmosphere. Infact, for Mahapatra, *darkness* has a great deal of psychological import as he grew up in the dismal darkness of his not-so-happy childhood house surrounded by tall deodars which instilled strange fears in him. The memory of his unsympathetic and non-cooperative mother, moving about with an oil lamp in her hand in the listless darkness of that house only intensified his fears further. Thus, *darkness* became an early childhood fixation in Mahapatra's life, which projects onto his poetry almost as a neurotic obsession, symbolising the fear of the unknown, uncertainty, a sense of entrapment and a host of other negative feelings. For example, in "Iron", Mahapatra says,

> A pain for the slight light at dawn
> assails me; dark earth,
> behind me still follows the darkness.
> Darkness from shadows under the roof and leaf
> [...].
> what branches of the dark will guide one home?[9]

This pervading darkness makes the poet acutely aware of himself, his limitations, frustrations and failures. Mahapatra can see through darkness into the abysmal corners of his soul wherein lie the dreams, aspirations as also the dark designs of unexplained guilt, fear and his inherent sexuality. The following lines from "A Country" amply illustrate this point:

> When darkness falls ·
> the old speak of the past with sleepy voices;
> my ears tremble when I hear their tales.
> I look at their faces, and their eyes are dead as stone.
> Here is my world, and it makes me dream as a child;
> yet why do I wear myself out
> feeling for the girls who die
> before their breasts are swollen with milk? (*Life Signs*, p. 29).

The darkness sharpens Mahapatra's sensitivity tough as it only results in pain and despair, and he dwells in the world of darkness with his archaic despair, willingly:

> I always return
>
> to the black world (10).

Mahapatra's poetry reflects, throughout, this swinging pendulum of his emotions: darkness represents the unfulfilled man, yet it is only darkness he wants because it throws light on what he has lost both as a poet and a man. The projection of this despair is of course, significantly, without self pity. However, because of the contrasting emotions, darkness actually remains unmediated, or its mediation takes place only at the level of imagination. Darkness thus becomes Mahapatra's meditative ground, which directs him to look inward, the way people often see, closing their eyes in a mood of deep contemplation or prayer, focusing their whole attention on one single aspect of their meditation. Mahapatra offers a wide spectrum of darkness for introspection, providing diverse points of view. This is the reason why Mahapatra's poetry does not have one single dominant mood, motif or theme. For example, the following lines taken from the volumes *Burden of Waves and Fruit* and *Temple* show the degree of variance of Mahapatra's mood, attitude and perspective:

> hungry for darkness
> by what I do not know
> ("Love Fragment", *Burden of Waves and Fruit,* p.34).
>
> Here, in familiar darkness,
> With its queer tenderness staying in the veins,
> The past becomes beautiful because it faces us
> ("The Year's Last Evening", *Burden of Waves and Fruit,* p.59).
>
> And
>
> the tormented cry of eternal darkness
> on the slopes of the Hill of Morals,
> the stubborn drone of bluebottles of a land's defeat,
> the voice of her father's daughter
> which guides her life,
> this voice of the builder of the unimaginable –
> and in the whirling embrace of her *laxman-rekha*
> she sees all purpose elude her and disappear.
>
> Her father, brothers all move with the sadness of men.

They belong, but not to her.
What could they say
after she had been raped
and left to her fate? (*Temple,* p.28-29).

Infact, the above quotations illustrate the constant shifts in focus which is characteristic of Mahapatra. It also represents the unsettled mind of the modern man and his troubled world of conflicting values, shattering faiths, unshared inheritance and the absence of a common destiny that all can believe in.

All great art have tried to enrich life by giving meaning and purpose to the existence of man. Mahapatra too has tried to do the same in his poetry through his encounter with the past; the past of the once glorious Orissa. Mahapatra strongly believes that man is but a link in the Time-continuum and the present is only a fleeting moment and becomes, before one realises, a moment of the past. Hence, this past is an inseparable part of our lives. For example, in "The Rising", Mahapatra says,

There is a past which moves over

the magic slopes and hamlets of the mind,

whose breath measures the purpose of our lives (*The False Start,* p. 44).

Therefore, Mahapatra strongly believes that his present is only an extension of the past, and his contemporaneity has its roots in the past which is not lost in Time:

And a man begins to begin again
In the centre of this past,
And sees no end of it ("Samsara", *A Rain of Rites,* p.8).

Hence, in Mahapatra, the past loses its remoteness and with this realisation the poet ponders over the essence of the past, its mysteries, myths and rituals which have survived till date. There is a constant attempt to relate the two worlds – the past and the present – in order that each may trigger a response, together forming an unbroken continuum.

Mahapatra does not glorify the past, nor does he revel in the present. The cultural and social past of Orissa and Mahapatra's individual past are intricately connected with each other in his poetry. Past thus becomes the shaping influence in Mahapatra's poetry, which gives the present an urgency and a sense of relatedness and belonging only with the past. His present is doomed by unrelated ness to relate with the external world because all such attempts end in pain and a sense of hurt. This perhaps, compels him to dwell in the past and see the present and future as time continuum, thus wiping out the categorisation of Time as past, present or future. This provides him with a *philosophical* framework to work out his dilemmas and ground them against the sequence of passing time.

Mahapatra's strength lies in his profound understanding of the socio-cultural heritage of the land of Orissa from times immemorial to the present day. Since Orissa, both as a specific cultural entity and as a typical part of India, forms an integral part of Mahapatra's poetry. Two aspects of Orissa seem to have had a dominant influence in shaping Mahapatra's poetic sensibility, firstly, the eventful historical past; and secondly the all pervading presence of religion with its roots buried deep in the mysterious tribal culture and the seemingly unchanging life-style of the Oriyas in general, which is by and large dependent on agriculture.

Therefore, in Mahapatra's poetry what we often encounter is the permanence and changelessness of a society, which draws sustenance from age old tradition, myths, and legends. Hence, Mahapatra says,

> ORISSA IS A LAND of repose, of faith and dream, basking in the tropical sun, caressed by the wind and the rain, its precious tranquility contained in its songs and its stones, and pervading its social and

> cultural fabric. Each season unfolds the earth to its way of peace, and the earth reveals its secrets again and again. Never and nowhere does Orissa make one feel alone. For agriculture is so closely bound to religion that it must needs give the people a purpose in life, so they can face themselves to bring them back to their earth (*Orissa,* p.8).

Therefore, Mahapatra's poetry becomes strikingly different from that of his contemporaries, the posts of the metropolis, whose major concerns are alienation, rootlessness, shattered beliefs and faiths. But Mahapatra has clung to his land and its ethos, and is passionately involved with Orissa which eventually becomes a potent symbol of metareality in his poetry. Yet, Mahapatra is not lost in nostalgia for the once glorious Orissa; instead his contemporaneity lies precisely in bridging the past and the present meaningfully and acknowledging the debt of the past which renders richness and significance to the present. Orissa, with its dense forests, rolling river valleys and coastal plains, its changing style of seasons, the incessant rain during the monsoon, the farmers labouring in the paddy-fields, their clay-walled, thatched huts and the countless temples and the festivals – never ceases to excite Mahapatra's poetic imagination. Besides Orissa, known as Kalinga Desa in ancient times, was known for its maritime activities; and its sea trade extended to Sri Lanka, Indonesia and the Philippines.

> A favourable sea coast with prominent ports such as Tamralipti, Paloura and Pithunda helped Kalinga in the establishment of a rich maritime trade; control of these ports and trade routes could easily have been one of the reasons why the Emperor Asoka invaded Kalinga [. . .].
>
> Defeat after defeat followed the Oriyas [. . .]. the most heart-rendering one inflicted by the Mauryan Emperor, Asoka, a defeat from which the kingdom never really appeared to recover [. . .].

> The year 261 BC denotes a bloody landmark in the history of Orissa. It is impossible to forget the carnage, the waters of the river Daya turning a gory red with the blood of the dead. Asoka, silent about his campaigns and the fate of the royal lineage of Kalinga, has given vivid accounts of the horrors of the war, in which 150,000 were taken to prisoner 100,000 were slain and many times that numbered killed in the ensuing famine and pestilence. One cannot but be moved when one reads the Rock Edicts of Asoka – not merely a historical record but a dreadful, tragic epic (*Orissa,* p. 12-13).

Mahapatra's poetry contains many references to this bloody war and Mahapatra *lives* that horrible experience as if he were both the conqueror and the conquered. This is only an example of how an instance of history descends into the poetic consciousness of Mahapatra as an intensely lived experience. On the other hand, we see the Sun temple of Konarka and the Lord Jagannath Temple of Puri, the two monumental creations of superb architectural splendour and artistic beauty, evolving as perennial symbols of man's destiny in all its rich complexity in the poetry of Mahapatra. Above all, the traces of the mysterious ancient tribal culture (especially the meria = human sacrifice), the tantric cult and rituals too become an integral part of Mahapatra's Oriya sensibility. Mahapatra's poetry shows unmistakable evidence of religious symbolism, which develops into metaphors of man's eternal quest into the mysteries of Life and Nature.

> Orissan culture has been influenced to a considerable extent by the aboriginal, and it is common knowledge that folk and tribal elements are an integral part of Hindu ritual and living (*Orissa,* p. 32).

Therefore, the socio-cultural heritage of Orissa is the driving force of Mahapatra's poetry and also is an aid to unravel the mysteries of his poetic creation. No doubt it has been a long, untiring but an equally rewarding journey, which takes Mahapatra not only through the landscape of Orissa but to its very *being* where beats the pulse of all that Orissa means and stands for:

> MY ROMANCE with Orissa should have begun with my birth, but I have little recollection of those early days. The period of my long memory begins on a warm afternoon when I was five: my father rushing into the house to hoist me into his arms and carry me to safety to the open grounds beside the 'Nanda Deul', the Naked temple by the Kathjodi river, as the rumble of an earthquake slowly subsided. From then on my life has appeared to echo with the river's murmurs and the temple's bitter-sweet bell (*Orissa*, p. 38).

On the other hand, Mahapatra is not blind to the merciless massacre of thousands of Oriyas in the bloody Kalinga War and the subsequent change of mind of the emperor, Asoka the Great, who left his rock-cut-edicts of peace for posterity. The present is a "mysterious inheritance" of that splendid past of "broken empires and of vanquished dynasties", where the conqueror and the conquered stood on an equal footing as they both contributed their mite, each in his own way, to the birth of a new dawn of Peace, though Peace was neither their intention nor the aim, but which incidentally became a valuable by-product.

> The invaders walk along the only road they know
>
> That leads to their bloody victories. (14)

This is one of the fine ironies wrought by history where bloody wars resulted in long interregnums of peace and tranquility; in the specific instance of the Kalinga War, that Emperor Asoka, moved by the ravages caused by the war, turned to the compassionate teachings of the Buddha and helped to promote Buddhism in the Far East. Society moves forward by the dynamics of history which always leaves its indelible marks on the lives of men and matter alike without offering a choice between a willing acceptance and an arrogant, outright rejection of its consequences. Any significant change generally has an unpleasant past, a painful history. Mahapatra constantly digs up the graves of history and attempts to give voice to history's stifled cries in a series of poetic encounters with the *ghosts* of history. Moreover, for Mahapatra, history is not merely a chronicle of the past but it is continually entrapped in the racial memories we so effortlessly inherit. Therefore, history becomes an integral part of our personality, may be its ghosts are buried in the subconscious layers, but nonetheless history has the potential to be revived by recollection. Or, even a contemporary parallel situations, in disguised form can still recall the dreadful past. Therefore, we can say that in Mahapatra's poetry the past evolves as a conscious, constructive and evaluative presence, which renders Mahapatra a significant poet in Indian poetry in English.

Silence is eloquent in Mahapatra's poetry. The reverberating Silence is rendered qualitative because it guides both the poet and the reader to meditate on the quality of human life. Hence, silence is not a state of speechlessness but becomes creative and meaningful. Sitakanta Mahapatra, the Oriya poet, too, speak of the brooding silence that echoes throughout the landscape of Orissa, from the influences of which no sensitive writer can escape.

> A visitor to Orissa can go to the Sun Temple at Konarka, the Raja-Rani at Bhubaneshwar, and many other exquisite temples at Bhubaneshwar, Puri and elsewhere in the state and listen to the voices of silence speaking from the stones. A glorious tradition of at least fifteen centuries of plastic art speaks through them.[10]

Hence, silence becomes the landmark of an integrated Oriya sensibility. Jayanta Mahapatra voices this silence forcefully: he expands its scope by infusing his personal sense of loss, despair and agony, which conveys his estrangement from the cultural matrix of the Orissa he desperately tries to relate and belong. K. Ayyappa Paniker says,

> The poet achieves his eloquent through silence. Silence, incidentally, is a word that gets endlessly repeated, one might say consecrated, in Mahapatra's poems.[11]

In the poetry of Jayanta Mahapatra, *Silence* represents what is lost in a culture by the onslaught of modernity and also the mystery of the past: it also reflects what cannot be repossessed in the flux of time. The following lines from *Svayamvara* and *Other Poems* and *A Rain of Rites* compel our attention:

> Spring freezes on the window's lips. These which rang
> like bells once, assumed silence (16).
>
> AND
>
> And that sky there,
> claimed by inviolable authority
> hanging on to its crutches of silence (16).

Spring is the season of flowering. Here it "freezes" as in winter. The next image is of a "widow" who cannot "flower" and hence Spring has no relevance in her life. But, Spring "rang like bells once": this strongly suggests the once-vibrant-marital-life of the woman full of hope, excitement, consummation and fulfillment, which now stands silent. Hence, Spring "freezes" on the "widow's lips": The memory of a full-blooded throbbing Spring, now silenced, only intensifies our sense of what is lost permanently. Mahapatra's highly condensed, and metaphoric style communicates this sense of loss on a wider scale in the second example quoted above. But before that, it may be worth analysing the metaphor of Spring a little further.

Seasons are cyclical, i.e., change, growth, retreat for a while, and renewal is automatic in Nature. Mahapatra does not seem to accept the consequences that flow from the metaphor which is basically cyclical renewal. ("I hardly see Spring coming in", p.48). Obviously this is not true of rural Orissa, where the constantly changing cycle of seasons decides the life-style of its people. But we have to remember that Mahapatra is not a meteorologist, but a poet who reflects the value system of a simple, rustic life-style wherein widowhood, with an irrevocable finality, seals the fate of a woman beyond redemption and beyond hope. A sophisticated urban feminist would certainly refuse this premise that there is no life after widowhood; for some, it could even be a beginning of a new life after widowhood; for some, it could even be a beginning of a new life free from societal constraints. But in the context in which Mahapatra's poem is placed, it does not admit of any such possibility. It may be easy to accuse Mahapatra as the patriarch of status-quo, but the reality is that this is an instance which clearly proves how truly Mahapatra identifies himself with the ethos of his land – Orissa.

Now coming to the second quotation, we know that the temple at Puri is a living monument of a culture and also the epitome of religious beliefs. It also represents the mysterious and the inexplicable in the history of human civilisation. And the vast expanse of the sky seems to hold the key to this secret, yet, man is not allowed the grace to unravel that mystery, because the sky is crippled and is supported by "crutches of silence". This maiming of the sky is highly symbolic as it points to the gradual erosion of vitality in the culture of that bygone era and its weakening power to support and sustain those values enshrined in that culture. But fortunately the sky is not altogether incapacitated. It can still limp, hanging on to its crutches. Mahapatra builds up this contrast of loss and hope, through intricately woven symbols. This collage presents a plethora of encounters with one's own existence and experiences.

Mahapatra explores the nuances of such an encounter because this sky over the Puri temple wields an inviolable authority on the life of every Oriya.

Infact, centuries of beliefs, traditions and rites are all inseparably linked with it. In our understanding of the history, there is always an element of elusiveness which escapes us. Mahapatra uses an unconventional symbol – SILENCE – to represent the inexplicable which always remains a part of our racial unconscious and of course an involuntary inheritance.

Moreover, all meanings that we attempt to attribute, explore and identify in a literary work spring from the sub-text of silence, because all literary endeavours are experiments with words and word-orders; their collocations, juxtapositions and combinations once organized remain as a super structure which contains multitudes of silence. Our own experience, ignorance, prejudices, confusions, and a whole range of emotions projected on to that structure help us understand the sensory experience imprisoned in it. That is why multiplicity of interpretations is possible and more than one level of response exists. Mahapatra defines silence thus:

> Silence is a sort of idea in my work, which may come as a revelation, and perhaps it will come . . . as a result of living simply – not aggressively – and the mind begins to flow like water. Or perhaps silence is an opposite pole to this: I mean there's always something I have never been able to find, even in whatever I call my own – like a wife or son – let me call that my silence.[12]

Thus, silence stands as a symbol of the unattainable, unknowable and the inexplicable that has an undeniably strong presence in the life of all human beings: it leads man on his eternal quest after significance, an element that renders quality to all human activities in the face of uncertainty, frustration and gloom.

Door is another significant and recurring motif in Mahapatra's poetry, which keeps haunting him right throughout his childhood. Mahapatra's unhappiness springs from the fact that his uncomfortable childhood and loneliness is mainly due to a rigid Christian upbringing, with rules of his mother sternly imposed. And the Door of his childhood – house was a witness to all his sufferings. This front door which his mother always made him close before dusk with an iron rung, ironically, shut him in, forming a sort of a private prison; and shut out the unknown outside world and its air of freedom.

> I pass the Door beyond my freedom
> and glimpse my haggard face.
> I look for those who once
> protected me by believing in me
> when I could not believe in myself ("Doors", *A Whiteness of Bone,* p. 53).

Thus, the door became a symbol of suffocating captivity and confinement, a fearsome prison of body and mind. The absence of electricity in the house only added to the already depressing dim interior.

> Often alone, I think of this door of my childhood which served both as a refuge from the terrors of the outside world, and as an object which mutely went on to lock me in, offering me no escape. It became both a haven and a prison, and my mind positioned itself both inside and out.[13]

This mode of perceiving the reality as an inseparable pair of opposites is characteristic of Mahapatra's poetic style. Mahapatra remembers the emptiness of the house and the dismal winter wind beating heavily against the door which intensified his fear. He also recalls the frantic wailing of his pretty young cousin who used to come running to the house, impatiently rapping at the door in terror, to save herself from the blows of her drunken husband.

And how I used to creep up in the dark to open the door, the slow, cold anger rising in me, as I suffered from weakness at my own inability to change the ways of the world. (139)

This door, then made Mahapatra aware of his own helplessness, frailty and limitation, and became a fixation raising a psychological barrier.

> I know I will always feel the door, this door of my uncomfortable childhood until my death, until my consciousness is there. . . . It is hard for me to say why doors keeps on coming over and over again in both my walking life and in dream, and why it keeps on pervading the poems I have written through the years.[14]

It is strange but true that even the most silent, imperceptive and inconsequential objects of childhood too can bring havoc, upsetting the delicate psychological balance of one's formative years, crawling in to the subconscious and remaining there for the rest of one's life causing unknown nightmares.

> The Door is locked,
> and I am afraid, afraid of the first ray
> of sunlight of the ascetic's smile,
> at the doom of breathing behind (21).

Luckily, for Mahapatra, this otherwise disturbing fixation does not turn into a destructive malady resulting in psychological malfunctioning; instead, it provides the impetus for his creative expression. Now in the adult world of Mahapatra every door is kept open; he is hesitant to enter them, for fear that they may be shut behind him and he may find himself once again in the gloomy interiors of his childhood.

> On the dawn of a new year
>
> something is waiting for me inside the door

of my own house (49).

Yet the basic human curiosity to know what lies beyond the doors proves stronger: what Mahapatra encounters there, every time he passes a door, is surprisingly his own self, *the other within*, the other unknown till then. This becomes an endless game of hide and seek, recognition and disbelief, affirmation and negation, which is frightening and reassuring at the same time, appearing as a bundle of contradictions – that is essentially Mahapatra's unique mode of perception. Further, the preponderance of Hindu world view and its rich philosophical tradition in the poetry of Mahapatra help us to classify the operating sensibility as unmistakably Indian.

Time is the *leit motif* in the poetry of Jayanta Mahapatra. Mahapatra's poetic vision is projected in time-pattern or a time-scheme; it ranges from the minuscule to eternity. It makes an attempt to study how Mahapatra explores the metaphoric interiority of time in his poetry. It advances that Mahapatra's concepts of time, which is neither rectilinear nor circular or cyclical, emerges from the nature of his own existence, both as a human being and as a poet, constantly being confronted by morality-immorality and flux-permanence dialectics. The kind of ambivalence that issues from the poet's belief in time as being simultaneous while he himself, his own existence is being governed by the tyranny of a linear movement of time, marks the manifest richness in Mahapatra's handling of time as a theme of ultimate veracity.

The sense of a place in Mahapatra's poetry assumes no fluid status. It is distinct and authentic, it gives the poet an identity of his own. The vastness of an Indian identity primarily rests on the recognition of a specific regional identity. Mahapatra explains his sense of nativity and home bound vision as an Oriya poet writing in English:

It seems natural I would express myself as an Orissan, even though I write in English. My writing would go on to portray cultural values native to Orissa, not to the other regions of Orissa. And perhaps I have done just this in my poetry.

I would never be wrong if I said that my own poetry has been about Orissa, this land where I was born and have spent all my life. India is too vast a country for one region to know about another.[15]

It is therefore, interesting to notice the shift in emphasis form the national identity to a regional identity. Whatever concepts or attitudes one discovers in the poetry of Mahapatra, one would certainly notice that these are because of the influence of the Orissan culture. Mahapatra's concept of time and destiny has something to do with his native culture. Mahapatra sees time as mystery, myth, eternity and time as an embodiment areas of our dreams and the unconscious. Mahapatra's poetry is replete with the durational aspect of time in which he seeks to define his own identity in relation to the place and culture. Time, as it appears in the poetry of Mahapatra, is perceptible through the process of change that one experiences within the self and without. Mahapatra's preoccupation with time springs from such a perspective which compels him to look back with a sense of awe and wonder – awe because the past cannot be revoked and wonder because it leaves enough impressions on the mind to overcome the problems of loneliness, fear, death in the present. Perhaps, this way of looking at time has some bearings on what the Hindu thought holds high.

Moreover, Mahapatra tries to clarify the nature of time that affects or influenced both poet and reader in the context of the making of the poem and its reception respectively. Mahapatra's preoccupation with the fleeting nature of time, is evident from the very first volume of his poetry *Close the Sky, Ten by Ten*, even if these poems are experimental and attempt to discover a genuine voice and idiom. In "The Anniversaries" the poets seems to be lamenting over the "eventlessness" of his own life even on his marriage anniversary. He is aware of a "painful nothingness" sleeping between himself and his wife. But very soon, his sense of "nothingness" would change into devotion. It is, as the poet believes, the gift of time that one has to accept with humility. The poet's veritable assertion of the continuous flux of time is in itself a proof of acceptance of the fact the time, whether of nothingness or of devotion, always establishes, perpetuates and redefines the relationship between husband and wife:

> Yet every time a moment is established
>
> Other moments are waiting under cover
>
> To reason away the thin line of scar
>
> That joins our snake-arms. (*Close the Sky, Ten by Ten*)

In an early poem "The Report Card" it is the result-sheet that separates the son from his father, and the loneliness depicted here is that of the son. There is "the escalation of greed / locked within a father's bone" and "the fear of reprimand" in the child at his bad performance in his school. It is now the child who "empties" himself "into duplicity". This leads to a sense of loneliness in the child which is depicted in such vivid images as:

> a splintered mirror,
>
> a shred of silvered paper, or the torn hand
>
> from some clock's face, these his own. (*Close the Sky, Ten by Ten*)

But as years slid by, the son wears his father's dreams, caught in the net of the same possession. Mahapatra, while trying to show the change that has crept into him, harps on the time as a fascinating and intriguing instrument that has the ability to connect, restoring balance between things lost and won, between past and present.

Therefore, the highly philosophical nature of Jayanta Mahapatra's articulation of experience renders his poetry sufficiently ambiguous with rich suggestiveness capable of multiple interpretations. Mahapatra never assumes the role of a preacher, delivering his judgement from a high pulpit; he leaves it to the reader to arrive at his own conclusions. Perhaps it would be right to say that in Mahapatra's poetry, the primacy of reader-response is as much valid as the primacy of the text itself. Perhaps it is also true that no other poet in Indian poetry in English has ever trusted his readers so absolutely as Mahapatra does. This indeed is a measure of confidence Mahapatra has in himself and in the ultimate integrity and validity of his poetic expression.

REFERENCES

1. Quoted by Pushpinder Syal, "The Use of Language." *The Poetry*. 204.
2. King, Bruce. "The Shapes of Solitude." *The Poetry*. 2.
3. Mahapatra, Jayanta. "Face to Face with the Contemporary Poem." *Journal of Literary Studies*. No. 6, June 1983. 16.
4. Swain, Rabindra K. "Uncovering Lost Possibilities." *The Poetry*. 275.
5. Mahapatra, Jayanta. *Orissa*. New Delhi: Luster Press Private Ltd, 1987. 36.
6. Kennedy, Alan. "Written Rites." *The Poetry*. 80.
7. Daruwalla, Keki N. "The Parsi Hell." *The Keeper of the Dead*. New Delhi: Oxford University Press, 1982. 45.
8. Quoted by Niranjan Mohanty., ed. "Voices Behind the Wheel: Poets from Orissa writing in English." *Indian English Writing 1981-1985: Experiments with Expression*. R.K. Singh. New Delhi: Bahri Publication Private Ltd, 1987. 72
9. Mahapatra, Jayanta. "Iron." *Journal of Indian Writing in English*. 11.2 July 1983. 10.
10. Mahapatra, Sitakanta. "Oriya Literature: A Brief Survey." *Malayalam Literary Special* (Jubilee Special). Trichur: Kerala Sahitya Akademy 4.3-4.4 July-December, 1980. 109.

11. Paniker, Ayyappa K., ed. "The Poetry of Jayanta Mahapatra," *Indian Poetry in English: A Critical Assessment.* Vasant A. Shahane and M. Shivaramakrishna. New Delhi: Macmillan India Private Ltd, 1980. 103.
12. Mahapatra, Jayanta. talks to N. Raghavan "Innerview." *Tenor* 1. June 1978. 61.
13. Mahapatra, Jayanta. "The Door." *Times of India* April 17 1991: 1.
14. Mahapatra, Jayanta. "The Door." *Times of India* April 17 1991. 1.
15. Mahapatra, Jayanta. "Mysteries as Mantra: Letter from Orissa." *World Literature Today.* Spring 1994. 283-288.
16. Mahapatra, Jayanta. *Close the Sky, Ten by Ten.* Calcutta: Dialogue Publication, 1971.

3

Jayanta Mahapatra's – Social Commitment

Jayanta Mahapatra's poetry is essentially metaphorical in nature. His language of poetry depicts the socio-cultural ambience of Orissa, by the experiencing *self* of the poet. Naturally, the language becomes resonant, sophisticated and metaphorical by transcending the superficial meanings of the words and thereby becoming an integrated symbol which creates a new poetic stylistics. In "Another Love Poem," Mahapatra says,

> In a country drugged with its own image,
>
> I only find my way in metaphor (63).

Poetry makes use of emotive language, in which the single or the absolute focus is absent. What the poet intends then, is to create a whole set of highly evocative and suggestive symbols capable of multiple interpretations by bringing in a whole range of connotations to bear on the specific contextual referral in question. In modern poetry, it is highly subjective experience of the poet that gets reflected often in a densely textured poetic medium. Since Mahapatra has his own unique modes of perception, his subjective experience is camouflaged in symbols and metaphors creating a poetry of indirection and opaqueness. Mahapatra's poetry is grounded in the "inner world of his own making, a world spaced by his own life, of secret allusions, of desire and agony, of a constantly changing alignment between dream and reality", which is at once challenging and baffling, uncertain and ambivalent, amorphous and inconclusive.

Mahapatra believes as a poet that the specificity of Orissan culture itself generates the symbolic modes of perceiving an experience, which comes naturally to the poet for whom the landscape is inseparably linked with his destiny.

> I believe that a culture (of which I am a part) has its dreams, and continues to provide the symbolic terms of our experience ("Inaudible Resonance," p.36).

So the metaphoric mode in the image-oriented poetry of Mahapatra becomes the nucleus of his creative endeavours.

We have discussed earlier how *silence, door, darkness, etc.,* are used metaphorically in Mahapatra's poetry. *Rain* is another significant metaphor which gets endlessly repeated. In the agrarian society of Orissan landscape, indisputably, rain is of paramount importance. But for Mahapatra, rain becomes a complex symbol which is hinted at in these lines in "A Rain of Rites", where the natural functions of rain as known to the poet is discarded like spent-up-ashes:

> Sometime a rain comes
> slowly across the sky, that turns
> upon its grey cloud, breaking away into light
> before it reaches its objective.
> The rain I have known and traded all this life
> is thrown like kelp on the beach.
> Like some shape of conscience I cannot look at,
> a malignant purpose in a nun's eye [. . .].
> Which still, stale air sits on an angel's wings?
> What holds my rain so it's hard to overcome? (10)

Rain = Water = Life-giving source = a symbol of fertility is reduced to a "kelp", i.e., burnt down ashes. Rain has lost the regenerative power; instead, it turns into destructive lightning before reaching its objective – Earth. Therefore, one is waiting for the rain, with hope in the eyes, turns out to be a false promise which not only frustrates but causes the hopeful expectation itself to be affected with malignancy. Even the pious nun has a sinister look – "a malignant purpose in a nun's eye" and her conscience is no more clean: perhaps it has turned turbid like the rain-water that gushes through the muddy gutters in the streets. Since the nun is infected with unholy thoughts, the fairy angel, who probably brings in rain, suffers a suffocation in the stale air of polluted loyalties and cannot fly lightly, and therefore the sky rains wanton destruction on mankind. In such a context, mankind as a whole is destined to suffer the imminent destruction, and the blame rests not on the vagaries of Nature, or the wrath of gods, but on the inherent human weaknesses which seem "hard to overcome". Nature's delicate harmony becomes the first casualty of man's greed in all walks of life as his heart has "lost its light and meaning"(13). Therefore, the rain comes as heaven's curse on mankind without wetting the earth. In this poem two worlds of eternal contrast – sky and earth – are bound by rain which is a "linking process". The poet, in an interview with Rabindra K. Swain clarifies the significance of rain in the above mentioned poem, "A Rain of Rites":

> There are two things which connect human beings: what is above and what is below. The sky is above you and the earth beneath you and anything that connects earth and sky is rain. It is a bond you cannot miss. It has a process itself. It is a link. Therefore, rain is a linking process, and so, the very act of your living.[1]

In *Dispossessed Nests*, rain is equated with the blood that flows like a river occasioned by terrorism for a wrong cause.

> A little girl's hate
> is already

a part of her,
rain water splatters
like
her murdered father's blood (19).

This unsanctified blood of the innocent victims poses a threat to our national integrity, and wore still, for the very survival of precious human lives which severed leaving people perpetually bleeding their souls, as it were, for the havoc wrought in their lives by the wanton barbarism of hard-core terrorists drunk with the bloody wine of violence. Therefore, the rain and wind too seem to have gone insane like the people, kicking and cutting someone "without reason", as if the elements of Nature also want their own share of violence, to counter-balance man's hostile and revengeful attitudes towards his fellow human-being as well as Nature itself.

Somewhere the rain kicks someone
like an enraged feudal landlord,
somewhere the wind cuts a tender face
without reason like a mean whip (43).

Even the river-beds are dried because "rain doesn't wet the earth anymore" and men are busy nourishing "the music of blood"(46).

a dry river bed that shall be flooded
in the rains of our fabrications (46).

Since the heavens have failed us because of our own inhuman tendencies, rivers are empty of water. The dry river-beds shall now be flooded, obviously, with the blood of violence and hatred, like "the waters of the Daya / stank with the bodies of my ancestors" in the distant historic past (14).

Jayanta Mahapatra says that he uses *rain* as a symbol to connect the "two separate regions of the mind between what, perhaps, I understood and what I did not, (148). So this grey matter, *Rain*, makes him question why there is so much of misery, unhappiness and bloodshed in this world; and, as usual, Mahapatra stops short of answers simply because none else seems to have any satisfactory answer either. In an interview with Aruna Ludra, Mahapatra clarifies:

> Perhaps I've used rain as a symbol in many of my poems. In Orissa where I live, it's not only the rain, which, as you say, blesses the earth and wets the earth and wets the fellow land after four long months of summer. But, suddenly when the rains come, you know, every now and then, we have disastrous floods in the coastal regions of Orissa. I've seen the misery of homeless people lined upon canal bridges on slushy roads, on treetops. And I've gone there myself, taking students and teachers along with me, doing a little relief work in the villages for years. So rain is not just a purifying thing for me, not purely a blessing; it has its other side too. Sometimes, you know this rain doesn't wet the earth, and its that sort of symbol I have also used at times in my poems. There are certain things I don't know much about. My poetry has always been questioning, of trying to find answers, of being on the border between the known and the unknown, around the mysterious. To grope around the limits of life. So rain serves as some sort of a symbol in my poems that way, and differently too in different poems.[2]

It is not surprising that in the highly subjective poetry of Jayanta Mahapatra, ironic mode of expression is neither a dominant nor a preferred poetic device. Infact, in his early poetry, irony is conspicuously absent. Mahapatra plunges into the depths of his own *self* in his exploratory poetic journey to know himself better. Vilas Sarang in his "Introduction", *to Indian English Poetry Since 1950: An Anthology* observes:

> It is notable that irony and satire, which are the staple diet of the Indian English poet, play an insignificant role in Mahapatra's poetry (32).

It is only in his recent poetry volumes that we get to see some glimpses of Mahapatra's ironic mode at certain social issues when the morale of a society as a whole is at its nadir as seen in the poems *"In The Autumn Valleys of the Mahanadi"* and *"Learning for Ourselves"*, both taken from *A Whiteness of Bone*:

> The House
> on the main street looks insignificant although
> its mouth is slack with the piteous screams of the
> girl burnt to death last August in the room on the
> landing. An old woman cannot fall asleep denying
> emotion about it, and she lets her husband bury his
> head
> between her breaths in the thick knot in her throat
> [. . .].
> Even if another death is planned, it doesn't bother
> the sun or the government. Just someone's voice
> stranger than any other one had heard before, and
> as though
> one has ceased mourning much too soon and knows
> it, with the tossing of branches in the languid air
> (51).

And

> Last year on the bend of the Debi River
> the rape of a young girl
> shocked us like ripe mangoes
> dropping from the bare trees in winter.
> Last year her murder and dismemberment
> made us understand somewhat
> the trembling in the eyes of cows we see
> being led meekly to the town's slaughterhouse (60).

Here, Mahapatra alludes to the atrocious and shameful social evil of *bride-burning* by the greedy in-laws for the sake of securing more dowry. Infact, the dowry-deaths are on the increase and have become unfortunately the modern counterparts of the equally cruel and shameful *Sati* system of the past where a widow was, often forcefully, consigned to the flames of the funeral pyre of her dead husband. A mother's heart always hears "the piteous screams of the girl burnt to death" and naturally sleep eludes her as she is overpowered by grief and the mother's choked throat swells in the painful remembrance of her daughter's cruel fate. But who cares? The custodians of law and order – the government – simply *does not bother* even if more similar crimes against the helpless women are perpetrated, and the judiciary in its total reliance on proofs, hardly succeeds in bringing to book the erring culprits. Therefore, the cunning culprits lose all fear of persecution and become more and more barbaric and invent new ways of crushing mercilessly all the human values under the dead weight of their selfishness and avarice. Similarly, rape is yet another heinous crime that most often goes unpunished. The fear, the anguish, the helplessness, the shame, the agony and the pain of a rape victim are powerfully communicated in the analogy: "the trembling in the eyes of cows we see / being led meekly to the town's slaughterhouse": cow's misery ends at the slaughterhouse but a rape victim is condemned to live with her burden which is more miserable than facing death. What is profoundly shocking is our general apathy, callousness and the loss of our capacity to be moved by the burden of human misery that abounds in our society. Mahapatra laments over this insensitivity that has crept into the life of man as he "has ceased mourning much too soon." Further, in "*The Lost Children of America*", Mahapatra alludes once again to yet another similar shameful event:

> In the Hanuman Temple last night
> the priest's pomaded jean-clad son
> raped the squint-eyed fourteen-year fisher girl
> on the cracked stone platform behind the shrine
> and this morning
> her father found her at the police station
> assaulted over and over again by four policemen
> dripping of darkness and of scarlet death (26).

Hanuman being the eternally celebrated God, nothing can be more ironical than the rape of a fishergirl in that temple, that too, by the son of the temple priest who has turned *modern* deviating from the traditional role and piety expected of his lineage. The victim of rape is a fisher girl who belongs to a low caste in the social hierarchy and wronged by a man of the high caste to which the priest's son belongs. Hence, the girl's meek protests go unheard. It is a cruel refinement of irony that even the police station where protection is expected is no better than the sinister temple; and thus the unfortunate girl has to suffer a similar ordeal of violation of her chastity by the four policemen, the so called guardians of law and order. What strikes us as important, even in depicting such a shocking, shameful event, is Mahapatra's controlled tone, which does not allow the poem to be reduced to a slogan of protest or publicity that could rouse easily the frenzy of a mob. Instead, the experience sinks, quietly into the reader's heart, touching him deeply, stirring "the echoes of a bruised presence [. . .]. / at the bottom of the soul's clear pool"(27).

Mahapatra's irony is not a pungent remark or a comment and is never biting, bitter or sharp; it never borders on sarcasm or takes cover under witty statements. Daruwalla's biting sarcasm and devastating irony provide a perfect contrast to Mahapatra's style. In the following lines, Daruwalla comments on the detestable vice of avarice that dehumanizes people by crippling their morale even in the face of a calamity like the outbreak of an epidemic or a war, which serves as a gold mine to the greedy to amass wealth by unfair and unethical means.

> If we had plague
> Camus-style
> and doctors searched for the virus
> there would be black-market in rats.[3]

Irony in Mahapatra's poetry, when present, is always

subdued, almost like a private whisper that invariably leads to self-introspection, being directed move towards himself, focusing on his own limitations and shortcomings both as man and poet. And it does not function as an intended therapeutic dose administered to improve the lots of a sick system, nor is his irony aimed at warning people who have gone astray, in the manner of a spirited missionary, to mend their ways lest evil befall them. Thus, we always see Mahapatra himself at the centre of his poetry, whether ironical or not.

"A Missing Person", "Hunger", "The Whorehouse in a Calcutta Street", "30th January 1982: A Story", and "The Twentyfifth Anniversary of a Republic: 1975" are the classic examples of Mahapatra's poetry as social commitment. Here, we may observe how irony, though mute in the characteristic style of Mahapatra, renders an intensity and immediacy to the experience handled in the specific contexts of his poetry, that its communicability improves remarkably. At the same time, the poems lead to the realisation of human predicament entrapped in the complex web of social pressures which, infact, act as serious constraints on the choices open to an individual to lead his life in accordance with his personal preferences. Thus, an individual's freedom is crippled and is made subservient to the demands of social pressures which dictate his fate. Mahapatra's poetic voice becomes sad and heavy when he deals especially with women's issues. He feels deeply for the plight of Indian woman who bears the burden of her womanhood in the utter loneliness, helplessness, humiliation, deprivation and often deplorable degradation. In "Hunger", Mahapatra depicts one such incidence. The poem is quoted in full:

> It was hard to believe the flesh was heavy on my back.
>
> The fisherman said: will you have her, carelessly,
> trailing his nets and his nerves, as though his words

sanctified the purpose with which he faced himself.
I saw his white bone thrash his eyes.
I followed him across the sprawling sands,
my mind thumping in the flesh's sling.
Hope lay perhaps in burning the house I lived in.
Silence gripped my sleeves; his body clawed
at the froth his old nets had dragged up from the seas.
In the flickering dark his lean-to-opened like a wound.
The wind was I, and the day and night before.
Palm fronds scratched my skin. Inside the shack
an oil lamp splayed the hours bunched to those walls.
Over and over the sticky soot crossed the space of my mind.
I heard him say: my daughter, she's just turned fifteen...
Feel her. I'll be back soon, your bus leaves at nine.
The sky fell on me, and a father's exhausted wile.
Long and lean, her years were cold as rubber
she opened her wormy legs wide. I felt the hunger there,
the other one, the fish slithering, turning inside (44).

Poverty and sexuality play havoc in the life of man and women debasing them to sub-human levels: a father is prostituting his girl-child, hardly out of her teens, luring a prospective customer in casual business-like manner that is most shocking. It is the stark poverty that has driven the fisherman takes refuge in "trailing his nets and his nerves" which indicates his disturbed psychological state of mind where an unresolvable conflict is going on. The fisherman is restless, and nervous; perhaps it is the first time that he is forced to sell his daughter. He is perhaps unable to reconcile himself to the bitter reality and his helplessness prods him on the unpleasantness of his atrocious act; yet the *father* in him prompts the fisherman to caution the customer against being rude to the girl-child. The fact that she still is a small girl is stressed by the line "she's just turned fifteen." And the father's concern is registered in these lines: "Feel her. I'll be back soon, your bus leaves at nine." Infact, "Hunger" is "a profoundly human document"[4], which contains within itself the stifled cries of countless innocent victims who fall an easy prey to situations, driven as they are by terrible hunger to become the objects for satiating the hungers of the flesh. Between the two hungers, these unfortunate men and women lose all dignity of their human person and live like mere shadows dragging their uneventful, burdensome lives from one day to the other, being resigned to their cruel fates, with no hopes of ever seeing a better dawn. Thousands of men and women are unfortunately condemned to endure this sickening life. Commenting on this poem, K. Ayyappa Paniker says,

> On the level of art, the local and the universal must meet. This is what we find in Mahapatra's famous poem "Hunger". The simplicity and strength of this poem has made it one of the great peaks of Indian poetry in English. A profoundly human document this poem is; and its power depends on the authenticity of the experience established by the words and their arrangement. Every word is telling, is in its proper place. One could hardly wish to upset any sequence in it. The happy blending of the literal and the metaphorical is achieved in experience like "the flesh was heavy on my back", "trailing his nets and his nerves", "the white bone thrash his eyes", "burning the house I lived in", "the flickering dark", "his lean to opened like a wound", "a father's exhausted wile", "her years were cold as rubber", etc. The protagonist, the fisherman and the girl have the clarity and hardness of figures in bas-relief. The complexity of the human situation is not sacrificed for the sake of any sociological formula (102-103).

In this context, the protagonist too is a victim of

hunger, i.e., his own inherent sexuality which forces him to seek pleasures in the ramshackle hut of a poor fisherman. The protagonist is also in a dilemma as to whether he should proceed or retreat. His moral world crumbles heavily on him. He feels that "the sky fell on me" and realise that "Hope lay perhaps in burning the house I lived in". Yet he follows the fisherman, unable to restrain himself and "inside the shack", two *hungers* confront each other, each as powerful and compelling as the other. Both the protagonist and the girl are victims of their respective hungers: both are losers: the protagonist loses his moral certitude and the girl, her chastity. Above all, human dignity becomes the first casualty in this whole process, which shatters the self-respect of an individual. This is no less destructive and damaging to the human person than an attempted suicide. Mahapatra says:

> The poem is based on a true incident: it could easily have happened to me on the poverty-ridden sands of Gopalpur-on-sea. Often have I imagined myself walking those sands, my solitude and my inherent sexuality working on me, to face the girl inside the dimly-lit palm-frond shack. The landscape of Gopalpur chose me, and my poem. To face perhaps my innerself, to see my own debasement, to realise my utter helplessness against the stubborn starvation light of my country.[5]

"The Whorehouse in a Calcutta Street" reads more like a sequel to "Hunger" but less successful than "Hunger." Nevertheless, the hollow world of prostitutes, the moral hesitancy of the protagonist, his frustrations and the same inviting business-like tone that tempts the protagonist continue to be essence of this poem too.

> Walk right in. it is yours
> Where the house smiles wryly into the street [. . .].
> Are you ashamed to believe you're in this? [. . .].
> You fall back against her in the dumb light,
> trying to learn something more about women

> while she does what she thinks proper to please you,
> the sweet, the little things, the imagined;
> until the statue of the man within
> you've believed in throughout the years
> comes back to you, a disobeying toy
> and the walls you wanted to pull down
> mirror only of things mortal, and passing by;
> like a girl holding on to your wide wilderness,
> as though it were real, as though the renewing voice
> tore the membrane of your half-woken mind
> when, like a door, her words close behind:
> "Hurry, will you? Let me go,"
> and her lonely breath thrashed against your kind (17-18).

The protagonist thinks that he can "learn something more about women" in the whorehouse whereas the prostitute goes about playing the tricks of her trade which is "an old, hard tradition" (30) and "does what she thinks proper to please" the customer without being moved by any feelings. For her, every new customer means only more business.

> The plump whore he has just left
>
> has brazenly gone to work on a new customer (18).

The whore cannot afford to have any emotional involvement either with the customer or with the act. That is why she is impatient and hurries the customer through the act of sex – "Hurry, will you? Let me go,". The sex-act becomes unsatisfying because the whore offers her body as a ware and not her heart. She tricks the customer into a quick orgasm and the protagonist walks out of the house more frustrated, disappointed and ashamed of himself: "the statue of the man within / you've believed in throughout the years back to you, a disobeying toy." In an interview with Aruna Ludra, Mahapatra asserts,

> My poems deal with my place, my people, my own people [. . .]. Much of the writing I'm doing right now, more or less deals with the socio-political processes that have been happening in our country. So I would say that I'm beginning to talk about things that concern me – about the Punjab problem, about poverty in my part of the country which remains as it was 45 years ago, about the continuing sexuality that bugs our people (54).

This clearly shows the shift Mahapatra's recent poetry has taken from a highly subjective personal world towards articulating problems that concern most people. However, it is important to note that Mahapatra depicts the baneful social realities with a high degree of objectivity which guards him against cheap sentimentalism.

In "30th January 1982: A Story", Mahapatra indirectly alludes to the heinous crime of murdering the Father of our Nation Mahatma Gandhi on the 30th January 1948. In the decades that followed the assassination, little has changed in the attitude of the people who have remained passive, selfish and petty in their thinking and deeds. No sacrifice is too great for such a people and the martyr's blood has not redeemed the country.

> Another day. Like any other.
> The bleating goat on the butcher's block
> quickened its last breath and stared wide-eyed.
> Its cry bent deeper still over the fringe of its death
> while the butcher worried that his knife
> was fast losing its sharpness.
> At this moment the mobile loudspeaker van
> of the Department of Public Relations swept past
> pouring out the words of Gandhi's once-favourite
> hymn.
> The rich woman cursed the Government
> for walking her up so early when it was not even
> fully light.

> The sunlight stole slowly to the fallow fields
> where village women were relieving themselves in the open.
> No one heard the cry ripening inside himself.
> Neighbours both, Amar Babu and Sham Babu smiled
> Sweetly at one another as they chose
> their choice cuts of meat hanging from the hooks
> in the marketplace. On a day just like this.
> As the scent of new mango blossoms blew in
> with the morning breeze, restless
> with the heritage of blood (26).

The political overtures of this poem are richly suggestive. K. Ayyappa Paniker certainly has a point when he comments on the turn Mahapatra's recent poetry has taken towards articulation of contemporary social realities.

A fact worth noticing about the more recent poems of Jayanta Mahapatra is that they appear to reveal an increasing concern on the part of the poet with contemporary reality with all its political connotations. From the preoccupation with timeless myths he has extended his range of interest to include reality. Still glimmering in the light of reason, not yet metamorphosed into myth.[6]

Godse killed Gandhi only once and we murder him everyday without remorse by recklessly discarding the teachings of the Mahatma. The "heritage of blood", unfortunately has been forgotten and we have become heirs to our own selfishness without any concern either for the nation or our fellow human beings. Can there be a greater than this? Our politicians are busy erecting monuments to the dead perhaps in the hope of themselves being remembered by such similar acts in the future.

> There are new statues on the crossroads, newer dead,
> that are visible from far and wide.
> The twentyfive-year-old-republic celebrations entertain:

> I paint my front gate in shiny aluminium
> and walk past it, to wait for the ceremonial parade.
> The bright winter light plays upon the silent statues
> of the dead.
> The destitutes everywhere are still my sense of guilt
> ("The Twentyfifth Anniversary of a Republic: 1975",
> *A Father's Hour*
>
> 19-20).

The country is so full of such public demonstrations of our feigned respect for the dead that there is hardly any place to turn without stumbling upon one or another monument. But nobody cares for the poor and down-trodden. Their plight has remained unchanged even after four decades of independence. This is the true, unhappy state of affairs in our country for which very largely, our politicians are to blame. Mahapatra's genuine concern for the welfare of the people finds an expression here,

> More than forty years have passed since we got our independence, and these years have failed to bring in the justice we sorely need in our day-to-day lives [. . .]. What about casteism, superstition, communalism and hunger we Indians suffer from? Is there any justice in those areas? And I ask: is there ever going to be justice in our life that we can flaunt with pride? [7]

In another poem "Summer", Mahapatra depicts a young girl of ten, combing her mother's hair – a common enough scene in any Indian house-hold – to reflect on the "impression of vastness" life holds for the two of them, suggesting their inevitable, but natural separation ("A Rain", *A Rain of Rites*, p.11).

> A ten-year old girl
> combs her mother's hair,
> where crows of rivalries
> are quietly nesting.
> The home will never
> be hers (14).

When the opportune time comes, the daughter will begin to lead her own life and when that happens, the daughter and the mother will meet on equal footing, the daughter having attained the status of womanhood fully. In our social customs and rituals, marriage has a very significant role. A daughter is considered as truly belonging to the family into which she eventually marries and it is her parents' duty to protect and guard her till such time. A father, while he marries off his daughter, tells the father of the bridegroom:

> Poornavarshatwiyam kanya putravatpalita maya
> idaneem tava putraya data snehena palyatam.[8]
> i.e., Thus far I have taken care of this girl like a son(without discrimination).
> Now that I have given her away in marriage to your son, let her be taken care of with love.

Viewed from this angle, "The home will never / be hers" assumes rich overtones suggestive of our cultural heritage. We may also note a faint tone of sadness that the house in which daughters are born and brought up with love, care and affection is only a temporary dwelling and that they have to create their own homes often among total strangers in equally new surroundings. At the same time, the attractions of her future life offer such excitements that a daughter looks forward to it inspite of her probable apprehensions about the uncertainties of that life. Therefore, Mahapatra says,

> In a corner of her mind
> a living green mango
> drops softly to earth ("Summer", *A Rain of Rites*, p.14).

Mahapatra's lines strongly suggest the irresistible romantic attractions expected of a happy marriage which remains a cherished dream of every girl. Infact, it is the celebration of life-forces that is manifested in all such aspirations in the hearts of the young, who burst with life energies in the freshness of their blooming youth. Nature is such a subtle conspirator that it catches the youth unawares and "a living green mango drops softly to earth" and that is how miraculous transformation take place in the mind and body of the youth preparing them quickly for the joys and challenges of a new life. Mahapatra's deceptively simple lines are thus suggestive of a whole range of emotions natural to the norms and ethos of our social life. Infact, Mahapatra is successful in universalising a human experience without consciously attempting to do so. His poetry is truly a metaphor of life with all its indeterminate, nevertheless realisable possibilities.

Mahapatra's philosophy of life may be summed up as his constant efforts to comprehend the basically incomprehensible in nature; this may no doubt look like a paradox, but that is how Mahapatra needs to be understood: opposites, contradictions and highly paradoxical perspectives and perceptions coexist in Mahapatra. Moreover, Mahapatra portrays the inherent uncertainty of human life and its predicament. This awareness makes Mahapatra restless, ambiguous and also highly creative. Therefore, the nature of his poetic probe into the essence of human life becomes equally complex and challenging in understanding of his poetry. Gary Corseri aptly remarks that Mahapatra's poetry is an encounter, which ultimately helps us understand ourselves a bit better.

Mahapatra's poetry is deep as the wellsprings of the human spirit. It cannot yield its riches to the casual reader. It must be mined and grappled with. It is poetry to return to repeatedly for the enduring beauty of the lines, the mellifluousness of the rhythms, the tapestry of images that envelop, startle and divulge our selves to ourselves.[9]

REFERENCES

1. Mahapatra, Jayanta. Interview. Rabindra K. Swain. *The Poetry of Jayanta Mahapatra: A Critical Study*. New Delhi: Prestige Books, 2000. 44.

2. Mahapatra, Jayanta. Interview. Aruna Ludra. *Indian Literary Review* 7.1-3 Jan, Apr, Oct. 1991. 53
3. Daruwalla, Keki N. *Under Orion*. 54
4. Paniker, Ayyappa K., ed. "The Poetry of Jayanta Mahapatra," *Indian Poetry in English: A Critical Assessment*. Vasant A. Shahane and M. Shivaramakrishna. New Delhi: Macmillan India Private Ltd, 1980. 103.
5. Mahapatra, Jayanta. "about 'HUNGER' and myself", *keynote* March 1982 n.p.
6. Paniker, Ayyappa K. "The Poetry of Jayanta Mahapatra", 113.
7. Mahapatra, Jayanta. Interview. Raja Rao. *Ten Indian Writers in Interview*. Calcutta: Writers Workshop, 1991. 26.
8. Bhatta, Vidwan Guru Krishna. *Sartha Shodasha Samskara Ratnamala* Kannada Tr., Perla Mangalore: Sri Kalikamba Vinayaka Devastana, 1991. 310.

   "Relationship: Vision of a Reconciliator," *The Poetry*. (Gary Corseri 185).

4

Jayanta Mahapatra – The Mouth-Piece of India

Mahapatra belongs to the group of modern experimentalists in Indian English poetry. His works seem to be attempts to link to the kinds of Indian reality. They also express conflicting concerns of modern life partially colouring them with his personal and immediate response to the world unfolding before him. They also seem to be introspections into the customary notion of reality. It appears he conceives a poem as an object having a structure of images and symbols. Images employed in his poems try to bring to the surface his obsessing memories, doubts and experiences which have been the source material of his imagination. He seems to be much intimate to the modernist movement of the first half of the century. The use of recurring symbols and his greater dependence on open-ended literary forms are endeavours to give coherence to non-linear, fragmented structures. Actually Jayanta Mahapatra's poetic art is not for the large masses, but it is meant for a small discriminating readership.

Mahapatra's poetry is the relationship of the self to the other, the distance felt by the consciousness between being aware and what one is aware of. As a matter of fact it is a central problem of modern poetry. In Mahapatra's poetry there feelings are intensified as he questions the existence of the self, the other often takes the form of local society, and especially Indian culture, ritual, spirituality, symbols and the part from which he has been alienated by his grandfather's conversion to Christianity, and his omen English education. In this poetry everything is problematic as Mahapatra observes his environment and listening quietly, sensitively to his inner feelings – the sources of his poetry bringing momentary perceptions of relationship and feeling images of contrite. It is a difficult, often obscure poetry of meditation recording reality as an unknowable flux.

This tone of quiet acceptance, with a latent awareness of centuries of suffering, perhaps indicates a very Indian sensibility. Some of the common themes in the world of Jayanta Mahapatra's poetry are: nature, seasons, women, temples, myths, history, time and sufferings. When we sees the whole range of Mahapatra's poetry we notice a wider variety of themes covering a large number of subjects like love, death, tradition, ritual and contemporary reality all attract him. But what gives an identity to his poetry is the breadth of his understanding, the temper of his mind and the depth of his vision.

Jayanta Mahapatra was born on 22nd October 1928, in Cuttack, Orissa. We need to look into some details of Mahapatra's personal life as they have a direct bearing on his poetry. Besides serving as a window to the poet's soul, give a glimpse of Mahapatra's unique style.

Jayanta Mahapatra's father, Lemuel, was a sub-inspector of primary schools. Mahapatra was raised in a lower-middle class Christian family. During the devastating famine that rocked Orissa in 1866, his grandfather, Chintamani Mahapatra,

> Starving and in a state of collapse, staggered into a mercy camp run by white Christian missionaries in Cuttack, where he embraced a new religion urged by the Baptists.[1]

His poem "Grandfather" focuses on this theme. There, Chintamani Mahapatra met Rupabati – a young girl from another village in Orissa who belonged to a different caste. Years later they married, and Jayanta's father Lemuel, was their youngest son. When young, Mahapatra experienced the pull of two religions. He says,

> as children, we grew up between two worlds. The first was home where we were subjected to a rigid Christian upbringing, with rules my mother sternly imposed; the other was the vast and dominant Hindu amphitheatre outside, with the preponderance of rites and festivals which represented the way of life of our own people. Two worlds then; and I, thinking to communicate with both, and probably becoming myself incommunicable as a result through the years (142).

This, conflict was further felt by the young Jayanta while doing his M.Sc, at the Patna University, Bihar.

I was utterly lonely those first days at Patna. Besides the differences, I experienced a huge cultural gap, I also realised painfully that I would have been subjected to unnecessary ridicule from other students in those lodgings had they know I was Christian (142).

Perhaps this fear of rejection is the cause for the near-total absence of Christian themes even in his poetry; Puri, Jagannath and Konarka have a dominant presence instead!

Jayanta Mahapatra recalls his childhood, his house, and his mother, both of which instilled fear in him – This fear was further intensified by his uncomfortable relationship with his mother.

I have never been able to feel that affinity with Mother (Sudnasubala, by name) as I had with Father. She was erratic in her ways, and as I grew up, my conflicts with her increased... I was flushed with tension. I didn't know what was important to me anymore... I slipped into dream. I kept more and more to myself. Mother did not appear to have any trust in me. It was difficult to agree with her (139-140).

> Although, he confesses "There are particular trait I didn't like about my mother, but I still looked after her till her death in 2003"[2]. After his M.Sc., Mahapatra joined Ravenshaw College, Cuttack, as Demonstrator in Physics where he fell in love with Runu who was doing a course in English literature. He declares, "Perhaps fate had decreed our relationship" (143).

Jayanta Mahapatra started writing poetry comparatively late in life, when he was in his early forties. His first two books of poems *Close the Sky, Ten by Ten* and *Svayamvara* and *Other Poems* appeared simultaneously in 1971, at the age of 43. So far, Mahapatra has published seventeen volumes of his own poems (to date, including his *Selected Poems*) five volumes of Oriya poetry, eight volumes of poetry translation from Oriya to English, two volumes of Stories, one book on Orissa and many articles in various journals, periodicals and newspapers. Some of his books are published abroad. For example, *A Rain of Rites* was published by the University of Georgia Press, USA, in 1976; *Relationship* by Greenfield Review Press, New York, in 1980; *Burden of Waves and Fruit* by Three Continent Press, Washington D.C., in 1988; *Temple* by Dangaroo Press, Sydney, in 1989.

Mahapatra was honoured with the coveted Central Sahitya Akademi Award in 1981 for his poetry-volume *Relationship* and he happens to be the first Indian poet in English to receive that Award. Also, Mahapatra is the first Indian poet to receive Jacob Glastein Memorial Prize instituted by Poetry (Chicago) earlier in 1975. Mahapatra has many distinction to his credit. Mahapatra was chosen for the University of lowa's prestigious International Writing Program in 1976-77. He went to Australia and Japan as

Cultural Award Visitor in 1978 and 1980, respectively. Again in 1984 he visited Japan as Visiting Writer and took part in the Asian Poets Conference. During 1985, he visited the erstwhile USSR as Indo-Soviet Cultural Exchange Writer. The Rockfeller Foundation Award enabled him to complete his long poem *Temple* as resident Writer, at Centro Culturale della Fondazione, Bellagio, Italy, in 1986. He was a Visiting Writer at Singapore Festival of Arts in 1988, and New Literatures in English Conference at West Germany, in 1989, and participated in the ACLALS Silver Jubilee Conference, University of Kent, Canterbury, England, in the same year. He has given a number of poetry-recitation programmes both at Indian and foreign University at their invitation. His poetry has been published abroad in prestigious literary journals like *The Malahat Review* (Victoria), *Critical Quarterly* (Manchester), *Poetry* (Chicago), *The Times Literary Supplement* (London), *Meanjin Quarterly*, *The Sewanee Review*, *The Hudson Review* etc., and *Chandrabhaga*: A Magazine of World Writing from Cuttack.

We can recognise three distinct phases of growth in the poetry of Jayanta Mahapatra: the early period from *Close the Sky, Ten by Ten* (1971) to *A Father's Hour* (1976) a period of apprenticeship, largely derivative in nature; the middle period from *A Rain of Rites* (1976) to *The False Start* (1980), a period of inventiveness and; the recent period from *Relationship* (1980) to *Random Descent* (2005), a period of profound maturity in thought and expression, deepening vision, contemplative mood and brooding tone.

Mahapatra's first two volumes of poetry *Close the Sky, Ten by Ten* and *Svayamvara* and *Other Poems* were simultaneously published in 1971, when he was 43, though he had started writing much earlier-at the age of 38. In the first two volumes Mahapatra's poetry show his restless preoccupation with language and the tools of a new medium in the process of formation. Mahapatra has no formal training in literature or poetry. He studied and taught Physics. Mahapatra's poetry of this period reflects a lack of unified vision. Expressions tend to be heavy abstractions without any pointers to indicate either their source of origin or intention. What his early poetry communicates is a sense of inadequacy of his poetic equipment; i.e., language seems to be burdened with alogical abstractions, free associations of ideas, juxtaposition of contrasting images, etc. There is little use of myths and symbols. It often consists of a heap of images, which are self-contradictory in nature, and the reader confronts them without any help which might guide him on to decipher the coded private experience of the poet. This poses additional difficulty which puts off any casual reader. Unless one is prepared to take risks of being constantly repelled by the increasing obscurity of Mahapatra's poetic experience, the private symbolism and its significance may not be easily accessible to a reader. Alan Kennedy aptly observes that "Jayanta Mahapatra is hard to read,"[3] and stresses the need to understand "Mahapatra's method".

However, the diction used by the poet in his early poems is not so difficult as it appears to be because of the frequent use of images and symbols which are traditional as well as personal. The poet suffers from a very serious flaw, i.e., in order to be innovatory he seldom uses punctuation marks that render him ambiguous and incomprehensible. In his first volume very few poem deals with some concrete situation, most of them are merely Mahapatra's experimental poems amply tell how his poetic skills develops and operates. They suggest that he never toils in the area of normal logic, but always in that logic of imagination as Eliot calls it, that he reveals in juxtaposing the abstract and the concrete, the idea and the emotion, the vague and the clear. The process of writing poetry, in his case, is a kind of adventure in the dark out of which he tries to explore something. Hence, Mahapatra's poetry is marked by originality mainly due to the reason that it has its own peculiar linguistic method. Very frequently we notice shifts in diction and syntax and recurrent use of favourite images is an integral part of his work in his writings. He has never been a poet of ideas though he does not rule out that the words should excite the imagination and bring some ideas to mind.

The poem titled "The Movement" deals exclusively with the creative process and has language as its main concern. The poet maintains a fine balance and control in the four well measured stanzas that show the process of poetic composition. It illustrates the slow and controlled rhythm that is one of the features of Mahapatra's poetry:

> as if to avoid a fall, leaning
> a word first in one direction
> and then the other, the white frame
> of thought proceeds with balanced skill [4] (p. 4)

The first line 'as if to avoid a fall, leaning' emphasises the tentative start that his poems have, then words like the legs of dancer first move in one direction, then in the other and then, by and by, the process of composition, like that of dancing becomes easy and balanced. Initially, Mahapatra used to start his poems with a small letter, but later on he gave up this practice. However, his fresh lines do not, as a rule, start with a capital letter except those following a full stop or a question. This pattern also corroborates his tendency of experimenting with the poetic form. This technique of using obsolete expressions in his poetry should not be taken to mean that he thrives on left overs, he rather uses them to give antique expression to his thought whenever and wherever necessary. Besides, it also suits his philosophical thought.

Whereas *Svayamvara* and *Other Poems*, Jayanta Mahapatra's second volume, makes the beginnings of his search for a poetic language more pronounced. The definitive norms of his poetry are in the process of their slow but gradual evolution. From a state of arbitrariness and linguistic-obsession in the earlier volume, they move to more concrete images and symbols. S. K. Desai rightly observes that "In the second volume, *Svayamvara and Other Poems* (1971), which consists of thirty-three poems, Mahapatra appears to move towards precision, by relating his craft more to the concrete than to the abstract, both in terms of theme and expression".[5] In this volume, we find Mahapatra's attitudinal change from a highly self-oriented private symbolism towards more general and contemporaries social issues. Now the artistic mediation through language comes off more naturally than in the preceding volume. This is surely a sign of a growing awareness of Jayanta Mahapatra's responsibility towards his craft.

In the next three volumes, *A Father's Hours* (1976), *A Rain of Rites* (1976) and *Waiting* (1979), Jayanta Mahapatra grows to be a poet of substance. The syntax and lines becomes relaxed. There is now something natural about the form and structure. The concrete physical details are coupled with an inexplicable sense of wonder and mystery "against or within" which he almost works, as Dick Allen aptly observes (35). These books, especially *A Rain of Rites* received high acclaim in US periodicals. Vernon Young said: "The manner of apprehension in his wonderful, sensate poems inevitably brings to the tongue the word, 'sophistication'. His psychology is at once more historical, more anxious, more involuted than that of any Chinese poet, old or modern known to me."[6] (627). Frank Allen praised Mahapatra for encapsulating "the paradox of Indias; both impeccable, both determined to dominate; the blank, shameless agrarian world with its polytheistic fatalism"[7] (340). These two worlds of contrast between "asceticism and sensuality, control and release, human and mythical ways of looking at reality" are manifested in the image of "Two gods copulating on the warm tar" ("Sunburst").

In contrast to the empty spaces in the heart of the early poetry volumes the poems of the late seventies are concrete with local details. The characters that crowd his poetry are typical of the Indian milieu. The poems in *Waiting* are more descriptive, more statement-like and clearer in terms of the emotional effect. The poem "Dhaulagir" named after the place of the well known Kalinga war is neatly worked out to question the adequacy Asoka's suffering is erasing the pain of war. Orissa is full of history – the temples, the sculpture, its rivers, every part is carelessly evocative of its past. Dhaulagiri (just outside Puri) with its river Daya: so named because of Asoka's remorse, is one of the most movingly historical spots in the world. However unlike other places in Orissa, there is nothing glorious here in terms of sculpture (beyond the rock edicts). Having long perceived Asoka's suffering as the raison d'etre of the Kalinga war the poem quietly re-centralies the thousands of men killed and wounded at Kalinga. Hence, the language in this collection is much plainer, the syntax less ambiguous, there is more punctuation and less fragmentation.

In *The False Start* (1980) the poems are longer and marked by a meditative mood; they address an unnamed 'you' and the poet achieves a unity of theme within each of the three sections into which the book has been divided. Vasant. A. Shahane writes:

> Jayanta Mahapatra, in *The False Start*, attempts to relate his life to his friends, to his land of birth, and more importantly to himself. The title is rather misleading (since it is not a false start). Yet the irony is quiet explicit, since the theme is, in reality, an exploration of the self.[8]

The volume has three section which deals with the

linear biological growth of the life from childhood to old age. First section largely consists of poems dealing with love, friendship, unfulfilled desires, absences, memories and secrets. In the second section, the poet enquires the purpose of our lives and the inability of grim reality to yield any truth. In the final section, the poet is oppressed with the devotees and hippies, desolate ricefields, fireflies, ancestors and ruins. Most of the poems are longer, the syntax is grammatically perfect. Images are expressive of darkness, decay and death.

However, James Finn Cotter feels that with the poems in this book the reader is "mesmerized," that the poems offer no "easy solution" and further that they move "from abstract to sensible imagery"[9]. The images like rain, cloud, moon, ash, voice and door are drawn from the very source of living in an intimate world and yet they are so smoothly internalized that the images transcend their physicality and point to spiritual and metaphysical perceptions. For instance, the door placed on the threshold of two eternally opposite worlds, gives an access to the poet to enter into either or both the worlds. In an essay entitled "The Door," Mahapatra traced the origin of the image of "door" to his childhood days and associated it with an inner freedom. The door

> Served both as a refuge from the terrors of the outside world which mutely went on to lock me in, offering me no escape. It became both a haven and a prison, and my mind positioned itself both inside and out.... There is always something very final, very secretive about doors (191).

Relationship first published by the Greenfield Review Press, New York in 1980 has undergone an Indian reprint in 1982 by Chandrabhaga Society, Cuttack following the Central Sahitya Akademi Award given to it for 1981. It is the first book of Indian English Poetry to have been chosen for this coveted Award. According to Professor K.

R. S. Iyenger, "Relationship is real achievement, for here there is neither 'Waiting' nor 'false start' but triumphant arriving."[10] In *Relationship* Mahapatra attempts to build a fugue-like structure aimed at evoking the myths and traditions of Orissa, and at the same time articulating the sensitive responses of his self to his spiritual, aesthetic as well as physical heritage and environment. This environment includes his own self his family life, his aesthetic existence and his responses to the hoary traditions of Orissa myth, legends and its rich architectural and sculptural treasures. It may be recalled that this book has been chosen for the Sahitya Akademi Award for 1981 on the recommendation of a 'final panel of advisers' consisting of Nissim Ezekiel, M. K. Naik and Ramesh Mohan. The poet calls it 'the theme song of my life.' According to Jayanta Mahapatra, "Relationship is a product of dreams, has made me speak of the demands of a pilgrimage – a pilgrimage threatened by the living Oriya past, by nagging hunger and a persistent sexuality."[11]

Relationship is based on history and myth but it has a vision. It has an epitaph in Eliotesque manner and the five lines taken from Walt Whitman unambiguously set the tone of it, in making an effort to unfold the mysteries of life. The poem is set in Orissa – a land of 'forbidding myth.' It is no collection of mere observation: a place here, a character there, but a determined, integrated set of sections built into the theme. Mahapatra insists on saying things and like any modern man who happens to live in an irreligious milieu, he is 'caught in the currents of time' and in his attempt to 'go into the unknown in me' tries 'to speak the myth of sleep and action' in order to soothe himself and others who suffer a similar fate. Hence, *Relationship* will be regarded as great poem on the basis of its meaning and the myth embodied in it.

If in *Relationship* Jayanta Mahapatra reaches the peak of his imaginative height, with *Life Signs* (1983) he comes down to the day-to-day physical world. The thematic concerns of *A Rain of Rites* is carried further in *Life Signs*. With *Life Signs* the poet becomes more simple and the poems becomes paraphrasable. The characters, events and objects that hold his attention are the contemporaneous ones, like the Western hippies wandering on "the dusty, malarial lanes of Cuttack" ("The Lost Children of America"), the women workers tarring the road in a hot summer afternoon ("Again, One Day, Walking by the River"), "Total Solar Eclipse," etc. In a lecture at Mysore, Mahapatra says:

> Governed as one is, as I am, by the unconsciousness – which in more ways than one acts like a power-generator, like a God – I would be satisfied if I can reveal a consciousness in my writing in agreement with today's realities.[12]

Among the Indian English poets writing today, Jayanta Mahapatra is one of the few who speaks of Indian landscape with the assurance of an insider. There is spiritual and moral degeneration everywhere. The plight of the people deeply moved him. The poet is convinced that India is a land of hunger, poverty, disease, casteism, communalism and many other evils. The poet's heart moans on these problems:

> My pain grows empty like the rainbow,
>
> It dances in the skeleton of the rain Limp with light.[13]

Mahapatra's poetry shows his concern for the society. That is why a rape here or a murder their upset him. He has devoted a full book, *Dispossessed Nests* (1986) to the hard realities that one encounters in our country in the present time. In an introduction to this book, the editors note:

In *Dispossessed Nests* one hears these wails of a world shattered within a human heart. Like burning rods of truth Mahapatra's poems branded the screens of our consciousness. In these poems we find deeply anguished outpours of an acutely sensitive man aspiring to capture a disintegrated world in the light of metaphors deriving their heat either form the torturous memory of the country's recent past or from a minute observations of the natural components.

Mahapatra is a keen observer of contemporary life and situation and does not mince words in describing scenes that diminishes humanity, in the country and the world around him in realistic terms. He 'sees life steadily and sees it whole.' Violence and lawlessness in contemporary society seem to disturb the poet. He says when the world around us seems to be out of tune, when good intentions fatally miscarry, can poetry save us? In a letter he writes:

I am uncertain as to what a poem would be, what it must contain, what it must say. But I have learnt to live with discontent because of the realisation that poetry has not helped the world to survive, poetry has not helped to ease man's suffering.

Mahapatra is basically concerned with what is enduring in the past and the relationship between past and present. How does man endure and continue to endure this unkind world? Will the world that absorbs love and goes beyond it, endure for all time? After relining the centrality of love in human life, he assents on his new identity of man's love in human life and he assent on his new identity of man, envision such a world where he can rise from the surrounding gloom and darkness and can identify the beauty and respond to voices of kindred souls.

In 1980s things have taken a turn for the worse so far as law and order is concerned. The anti-national activities in Punjab in the name of Khalistan and the Bhopal Gas tragedy have sent shock waves throughout the country. The blurb of the book rightly makes a note of it in the following words:

> Mahapatra unleashes the buried horror of long and supreme knives in Punjab and the barbarous dance of bejeweled snakes, of multinational companies in Bhopal. The poems are bitter experiences of the Indian masses betrayed by an inhuman set-up.[14]

Bloodshed, violence and destruction have become the hallmark of today's world. Death is the all pervasive force in *Dispossessed Nests*. Death is the only thing that lasts. Compared to the troubled State of Punjab all over states are by and large peaceful. The poet minutely observes it with a sense of fear and disappointment, indiscriminate killings have caused panic all over the country and humanity has lost its way into oblivion and hate reigns supreme. Man has degraded himself to the level of animals and 'jungle law' prevails. In these circumstances it is difficult to find a way out as things drift apart with the passing of each day. Thus, hoping against hope the poet wonders 'if this is the last explosion.' The senseless violence has robbed off man of his conscience and he depicts the horror of life due to violent Khalistan movement and Bhopal Gas Tragedy with a tone deeply imbued with pathos, the poet observes, 'the country we try to leave behind seems upset by its own silence' and people smell the danger that awaits them in future. Life has lost its charm as it is beset with danger and uncertainty.

If the happenings in Punjab and the Gas Tragedy in Bhopal make the poet sad, the brute massacre at Nellie in Assam breaks his heart. Violence occurred in any part of the country is reprehensible for the poet and he is responding to it through his poems like the Mouth-piece of India and when the world around us seems to be out of tune, when purblindmen enact hell, when good intentions fatally miscarry, can poetry save us? That's a million dollar question. Mahapatra tries to answer this question in his own way in "Last Night the Poem":

> But what use is a poem, once the writing is done?
> Words looking for what, in the dark of the soul?
> like the sound of a match stick striking, then over;
> I know that much. When all else has failed,
> the poem's words are perhaps justified.

This takes us to another poem titled, 'Will a Poem of Mine Be the Only Answer?' in which the poet states that a special kind of feeling he gets from his poems though they do not solve all problems. The world would have been an illusion to him without his poems. With Mahapatra, earlier it used to be the pure, uncontaminated inner-world, the socio-cultural and mythic details of the past and the pastness of the present economic and political world. Now, he constructs his poetic world on the bad news of the present rather than on the golden past.

The process of ageing and the problem of coming to terms with it through poetry becomes his agonising ordeal in *Burden of Waves and Fruit* (1988). His poetry, as has been already observed, is marked by his shuttling constantly, phase by phase, from the inner world to outer world and vice versa. As a result, he takes up the images from both the worlds: in *Life Signs* speaking of the lives and conditions around him he had made use of the signs of external world and now that he is back to his body in *Burden of Waves and Fruit* his attention is arrested primarily by the elements and working process of the body itself. It is distinct from his early works at least in one sense: most of the poems here deal with the theme of death. This volume is rather a creative attempt at relating physical decrepitude with moral disintegration and the breakdown of the spirit. However, conspicuous presence of death makes itself felt in the various manifestations of the poet's imagination. In this sense, this volume becomes a watershed in the career of Jayanta Mahapatra by distinctly marking a fundamental concern of an ageing poet, that is, the relationship of the self to the ageing, alienation, slowly turning decrepit body and the ultimate death awaiting it.

By the time this volume was prepared for publication the poet was around sixty. So it was natural that his poetry should have responded to the immediate and urgent demand of exploring the ageing body. In trying to meet this demand the poet turns the gaze of the "centre of your web" towards the inside of the body. Body, then, becomes the centre of attention as well as the centre of his poetic world and consciousness. The body now emerges triumphantly as an overpowering image:

> I touch my shoulders; they are bare, contrite.
> Like the shape of a deserted park bench in the rain. (52)

The shoulders of his ageing body are "contrite": they are "bare" "like a deserted park bench "in the rain." The signs of ageing on the poet's body are conspicuous, but "contrite." The body that has started holding his attention deceives his very self. Now that the body is slowly becoming a burden, intruding into the terrains of his consciousness, he is getting increasingly obsessed with it: "shoulders," which he might have considered obnoxious a decade ago, have replaced the heart. Of his heart he is growing diffident; sullen: "The heart has nothing to learn,"(39) whereas a decade earlier, he has said:

> Where is that absence which pushed an icy rope
>
> down my throat, so close my heart could have touched it?
>
> (*A Rain of Rites* 24)

The preoccupation with "absence," with "waiting," with a haunting sense of unfulfilment continues through these years. What has intervened is the shadow of ageing demanding for itself an exclusive attention from the poet. Further, his mode of giving shape to the immaculate feeling, and dissolving the existing shape of things into a flux, continues. Old age has come to him like a "weary night bird,"(51) like "a grey owl on a branch of (his) breath"(53). The presence of this bird is ominous. The soul is now about to depart like this bird and he is aware of its consequence: he will be left as "a soiled shirt as though it were empty of its body"(50). The indelible signs of old age make him feel that he is being reduced to a mere "symbol." His "poem taunts (him) like a discarded bone"(29). "The naked truth of ageing is that," as Kathleen Woodward says, "while we usually associate young age with arms and legs and reaching out into the world and old age with the interior organs, we think of the youth as the symbol of social interaction, while we think of the immobilized, infirm elderly as turning inward, preoccupied with the invisible working of the body's internal mechanism."[15](54) These reflection s on old age, as against youth, are abundantly, noticed in the recent poetry of Jayanta Mahapatra:

> Here I lie, watching
> the summer of my body
> trembling over the grass (12)

Here we find the poet watching "the summer of (his) body," instead of the exterior worlds of stars, sky and fullmoon night around him. He is preoccupied with the dark workings of the inside of his body. His gaze is inward, bodyward. "Grass," which is an image of youth and vitality, now seems to be merely a shred of memory, overlooked, existing on a different plain, a thing of the past. Where there was once suppleness and tone – "grass"- now there is dryness, "absence," loss of colour – "summer" (12).

In an interview with the Indian Express Jayanta Mahapatra says, "I have been working hard somehow feeling that I don't have much time left. The morbid streak you find in my poetry is also there within me. The idea of death has always been with me." (Sept. 5, 1987) Of course, elsewhere, he had already equated death with poetry: "it has sometimes been said there are two main things poets can write about: love and death. For in poets dwell Man, this biological being, easily hurt, easily destroyed. And if one thinks a little on this, one will come to the conclusion that in reality there is only one subject all poets talk about – and it is death." ("Poetry: Climate for Renewal" 7-16)

Thematically, *Temple* (1989) is a continuation of *A Rain of Rites* published more than a decade ago, in making *Woman* the central character and the focus of Mahapatra's probing spirit. The progression of the theme gains in intensity and depth of treatment. It starts with the news flash from *The Times of India* dated March 24, 1980, on the death of an Octogenarian couple Ramanujan (85) and Chelammal (80), who were believed to have committed suicide because of poverty and loneliness. This leads the poet to ponder over the plight of Indian women in general. Mahapatra captures, with rare insight, the burden of tradition on women at all stages of their lives. Their individuality seems crippled and is made subservient to the all-powerful and all-demanding, predominantly patriarchal system of our society. Chelammal becomes the guiding spirit in *Temple*, representing the collective consciousness and the collective psyche of women: she echoes the dreams, disappointments, ecstasies and sighs of every woman. Mahapatra ruminates over the permanence of the predicament of Indian Woman:

> If *Temple's* theme is the plight of the Indian Woman, urged by the opening news item in the ms, then there is reason to suspect little change, despite the seemingly dramatic changes depicted by today's media (57).

The volume ends with another news flash from *The Telegraph* dated January 5, 1986, i.e., almost six years later from the one quoted at the beginning, which states "A 12-year- old girl was allegedly gang raped and murdered... No one has been arrested so far"(*Temple*, p. 56-57) – which only confirms Mahapatra's apprehensions. Mahapatra eventually infuses into her spirit the strong Will of Putana who was prepared to die in the hands of Lord Krishna with the hope of deliverance from the cycle of birth and death.

A Whiteness of Bone (1992) contains fifty-nine poems dealing with a variety of themes ranging from landscape and time to the grim realities of the contemporary world. It encompasses topics like the Bhopal Gas Tragedy, Assassination of Mrs. Indira Gandhi and the consequent riot in Delhi and the self-immolation by fire of students protesting against the implementation of caste law by the Mondal Commission. Mahapatra's sense of patriotism and awareness of contemporary situations together give rise to his concern for the country. Time has brought a remarkable change in society. No longer the children are afraid of their parents. The generation gap has widened the credibility gap between parents and children. 'The wheel has turned a full circle,' and the parents are now very much conscious of their position.

Mahapatra creates poetry out of contemporary situation. He encounters everyday reality with the insight of a scientist and portrays it with objectivity of a true artist. In "Red Roses for Gandhi", Mahapatra tells us how we have forgotten Gandhi's ideals and relegated him to the background by observing his birthday to a mere ritual. The poem is occasioned by the immolation of eight students on October 2, 1990, the day of Gandhiji's birth Anniversary. Time has changed, we mechanically perform rituals on his birthday without practicing his ideals. Whereas, the poet comes down heavily on those who criticised Gandhi and pay only lip service to him and for these misguided people Gandhi has become a faded picture. So, in this volume he steps out on to the street and into the remote village, in order to express the poet's anguish about contemporary Indian society.

Shadow Space (1997) is Jayanta Mahapatra's fifteenth volume of poetry consists of fifty-four poems. It also illustrates the dark aspects of Orissa, and his disgust with himself for not being able to improve the situation through the medium of his poetry. He knows that 'I write my futile poems,' 'Poetry stumbles and falls' and that his poetry is as 'a river without water.'

Jayanta Mahapatra is touched by the sudden demise of A.K. Ramanujan in Chicago resulting in the birth of a poem, "A Day in Marburg on-the-Lahn." This elegiac piece will perhaps remain as a milestone in Indian English poetry. The poem is very much unlike Jayanta Mahapatra in the sense that it has no complex metaphors, no private symbols. Infact, like death baring life, any talk of death in poetry would strip its ornaments. The hearts of the two men as such, of two poets come to the open. Here is the portrait of two poets, the homage of one to the other, the scrutiny of one's self and on the whole, speculation on the ultimate silence. Here one is struck by the intimate sharing of each other's world:

> Suddenly you said you had something to buy.
> "Birkenstock sandals," you went on to say.
> I had never heard of this brand before. "They are
> the best, you know, Jayanta." I didn't.
> A Bata was all I knew. You smiled, as you rose... (47)

The two poets were meeting for the first time after twenty years since they knew each other. Even after that, they did not have any correspondence which speaks of the reticency and a lack of proficiency in pushing themselves forward. Says Mahapatra, he never wanted to ask Ramanujan "about poetry or peace or love."

Bare Face (2000) is a collection of poems prefaced by Camilo Jose Cela's words, "A beheaded puppet is a sadder sight than a dead human being." The volume is divided into two parts and addressed to his grandchildren Ayesha and Nikhil. First part consists of twenty-six poems and the second part entitled "Requiem" having twenty sections. In this collection Mahapatra is painfully aware of his past; memories, personal or as a legacy of burden, a journey backward through time in a dream-like state and of late Mahapatra's poetry has started assuming somewhat political overtones. In an article published in *The Hindu* Jayanta Mahapatra has ably dealt with the question. According to him, there cannot be any hard and fast rules, but poetry that ignore the historical relationship between the self and the society becomes lifeless. "The poet who does not see reality around himself is dead; so too the poet who 'only' sees reality around him." That is how he deals with the grim realities that surround him and scream for attention. A distinct feature of the book is that it contains a long poem on Gandhi in its second part. The poem is highly evocative of Gandhiji's life, times and philosophy which flows like a sentimental flashback. The poem bears all the marks of the typical Mahapatra's style of metaphors, powerful images of decay, deep melancholic voice, ironic rumination proclaiming louder than ever, that the civilised world we profess to inhabit is a blatant refutation of all that Gandhi stood for.

Random Descent is Mahapatra's most recent collection of poetry published in the year 2005. In this volume his poetry of non-comment turns to be poetry of comment. It is the poetry voicing his protest and intolerance against the sufferings of the poor, weak and downtrodden of the land. He wants to safeguard the poor sufferer and the women class at large. Divided into three sections, this collection of poetry is a fresh recurrence of the old legends, the poet was elaborating throughout the past three decades.

It consists of a total of forty-nine poems, which deal with the familiar characteristic like Orissa's architectural cosmogony, social turmoils, widespread terrorism and Mahapatra's favourite images of stone, darkness and light emerge with renewed possibilities.

REFERENCES

1. Mahapatra, Jayanta. Autobiography: *Contemporary Authors Autobiography Series*. 9. 141.

2. Mahapatra, Jayanta. In conversation with Rahul Mene. *UGC Sponsored National Seminar on "Indian Ethos in Indo Anglian Literature."* Durg: 21-22 Oct. 2005

3. Kennedy, Alan., ed. "Written Rites," *The Poetry of Jayanta Mahapatra: A Critical Study*. Madhusudan Prasad, New Delhi: Sterling Publishers Private Ltd. 1986. 74.

4. Mahapatra, Jayanta. *Close the Sky, Ten by Ten*. Dialogue Publication, Calcutta: 1971. 4.

5. Desai, S. K. "The Poetic Craft," *The Poetry*. 119-120.

6. Young, Vernon. "Poetry Chronicle," *The Hudson Review*. XXX, 4 Winter. 1977.

7. Allen, Frank. "Crisis of Belief," *Parnassus: Poetry in Review*. 9, 1. Spring / Summer. 1981. 332-41.

8. Shahane, Vasant A., ed. "The Naked Earth and Beyond: The Poetry of Jayanta Mahapatra." *Perspective on Indian Poetry in English*. M. K. Naik. New Delhi: Abhinav Publication, 1984. 153.

9. Cotter, James Finn. Review of *The False Start*. *The Hudson Review*. XXX, 3. Autumn 1982. 477-78.

10. Iyenger, K. R. S. *Indian Writing in English*. New Delhi: Sterling Publishers Private Ltd. 1984. 715.

11. Mahapatra, Jayanta. "The Inaudible Resonance in English Poetry in India," *The Literary Criterion* vol. XV, No. 1, 1980. 36.

12. Mahapatra, Jayanta. "Poetry: Climate for Renewal," The David H. McAlpin and Sally Sage McAlpin Lecture, A Dhvanyaloka Publication. Mysore. 1985. 13.

13. Mahapatra, Jayanta. *A Whiteness of Bone*. New Delhi: Viking. Penguin Books India Private Ltd., 1992. 59.

14. Yuyutsu, R. D. and Ramanand Rathi. "Introduction," *Dispossessed Nests: The 1984 Poems*. Jaipur: Nirala Publication, 1986. 10.

Woodward, Kathleen. "Instant Repulsion: Decrepitude, The Mirror Stage and Literary Imagination," *The Kenyon Review*, V, 4. 1983: 43-67.

5

The Problems of Heritage – Myths, Rites, Rituals

Mankind is continually engaged in a fruitful search for the right clues to unravel the mysteries of Nature. Through his varied activities man transforms Nature for making his life more comfortable and in the process he is also simultaneously transformed by Nature which creates a new awareness and also generates new needs and aspirations. Both these transformations are conditioned by the historical and social environments which are operative in the specific contexts of time and place. No man has freedom in the choice of an appropriate time, a suitable place or a favourable socio-historical condition to begin his life simply because he cannot choose his parents. A man is born into a specific socio-cultural milieu and he inherits, quite unconsciously though, and often without efforts, the accumulated wisdom of earlier generations in the form of traditions, legends and myths. Therefore, it is apt to say that "myth is the embodiment of human aspiration and its appropriate imaginative form".[1] No man can relate himself meaningfully to his fellow human beings without being nurtured by the myths which sustained the earlier generations.

Myths are the potent symbols of man's dreams and aspirations, which provide him with ideals and help him set goals in a hostile world that constantly threatens man's existence. Struggle for survival consume man's life energies and he needs fresh impetus to go on facing and tackling the new obstacles which keep propping up like the ending, rolling waves in the sea. Myths and legends provide mankind with the much required psychological support and help him discriminate between good and evil judiciously. However, mankind's history is codified in its myths and therefore myths symbolically represent what has stirred man's soul in his life's journey from times immemorial to the present day. Carl Jung, the well-known psychoanalyst, stresses that myths are indispensable for discovering one's root:

> If we are to see things in their right perspective, we need to understand the past of man as well as his present. That is why an understanding of myths and symbols is of essential importance.[2]

Each one of us is a part of the cosmos, the inexplicable and the eternal. The essentially religious spirit of man must have invented and projected myths that have sustained whole civilisations, interpreted the significance of life, connecting it with the unknown. The present has meaning only in relation to the past in a manner that the past was not aware of itself. As Sivaramakrishna says,

> Without roots in history and myth no poet can hope to make his aesthetic strategy other than merely cerebral [. . .]. affirmation of the environment and awareness of its mythical bases can hardly function in the absence of a pervasive personal quest of significant personal emotion.[3]

Jayanta Mahapatra attempts to explore the dark corners of the human soul to elicit meaning and significance of life. His attempts to penetrate into the hidden depths of the collective unconsciousness of human race by breaking through the mythical heritage of man. By correlating his personal quest with man's eternal preoccupations,

Mahapatra endeavours to define the predicament of modern man torn between conflicting values, shattered faiths, the lurking darkness both *within* and *without*, and a near- total absence of life-sustaining mythical values.

Mahapatra is haunted by a strange sense of fear and uneasiness throughout. In many cases the source of these apprehensive feelings is his own imagination without a correspondence, atleast the obvious one, in the external reality. Mahapatra himself reflects this sense of fear in "My Boy" taken from his *Svayamvara* and *Other Poems*:

> From where his fears
> come, he looked into and wondered
> at other fears, doubled in a pupal face,
> the secret signs of a tabooed race (32).

It looks as though these fears are grounded in the primitive consciousness of the prehistoric man, who being unable to explain the natural phenomena of fire, thunder, lightening, rain, etc., looked at them with awe and wonder. He came to regard these as manipulations of superior astral powers which guided the life and destiny of men and matters alike, the uncertainties of his nomadic life coupled with the equally unpredictable vagaries of Nature, left everything to chance in that primitive society, including man's very own survival. This certainly must have contributed to man's fear of the inexplicable in the universe and perhaps also roused his curiosity to explore, what he might have inferred to be a fundamentally more powerful but equally invisible causative factor. Thus, the primitive man came to believe in the mystery of the universe, driven as he was, by a strong desire to live and propagate. Naturally then he felt the need to appease these *unknown forces* to protect him from their potential destructive powers and also to seek their benediction to live and prosper. Mahapatra narrates the practice of human sacrifice conducted, till the end of the last century, by the Kondhs, a primitive tribal community which inhabits the mountainous tracts of south and west Orissa:

> The *meria* sacrifice, as it is called, can be looked upon as a part of the universal preoccupation of the primitive mind, seeking to propitiate the supernatural powers for the peace and prosperity of the entire tribe. Religious symbolism, obviously, was at the root of the *meria* sacrifice (33).

Thus, rituals and magic were devised which represented symbolically man's submission to the superior powers. Conversely, this ritualistic magic also became the means of man's quest to know, understand and interpret the nature of this mysterious power. This is how perhaps religion was born with its intricate system of secret signs and symbols, from the rudiments of man's fear of the inexplicable, the unknown and his curiosity to explore the unknowable. Jayanta Mahapatra makes an attempt to articulate these symbolic gestures of mankind's eternal search into the unknown through his poetry.

But Mahapatra's probe leads him into an exploratory journey unto the *self*. In the amphitheatre of his mind the burden of the whole race with its taboos, rites and magic is constantly re-enacted in the hope of understanding man in relation to Nature. In "Ceremony", Mahapatra explores the significance of rituals thus:

> What is there in ceremony, in a ritual's deeply hidden meaning?
> The familiar words are rude like roots, and out of place,
> hanging like history in which one's sky stumbles.
> In the world it is always I who come back to myself,
> that far flower of thought; the sacred cold books flash
> with star pyres[. . .].
> Any cult here, triumphs for ever (15).

Ironically, the gestures man created towards off his chocking fears have now come to be the source of generating new fears. The increasing complexity of these symbols, through their transformation and other associations gained with the passage of time has only drifted man away from the original meaning, purpose or message, imprisoning him tragically in the mess he has created for himself. Following lines from "India" deserve a close study.

> When we learned dumbly to grow,
> we felt of curselves abandoned in the wilds, in things not
> real,
> full of the mysterious fog that excites the shadows of the spirit (50).

Here, the word "dumbly" has a negative connotation which suggests that man has not grown at all. Therefore, he feels "abandoned in the wilds" without direction or purpose. This abandonment is made more fearsome because man is lost "in things not real" in a dense "mysterious fog" which blurs his vision. Nevertheless, the "mysterious fog" invokes something unknown to the phenomenal world. Therefore the "shadows of spirit" are excited and the prospect of a glimpse into the unknown seems brighter than at the stage before man's "abandonment in things not real." This ambiguity in responding to a situation is characteristic of Mahapatra's poetic craft.

For Mahapatra, no history of human civilisation will be complete without considering its rites and rituals which bind people together into an identifiable whole, as a community. A deep insight into the natural of these rites becomes compelling as it forms a vital part of the socio-historical background of Orissa, with its sizeable tribal population for example, the Juang tribe is only one of the sixty two aboriginal tribes, who inhabit the forest regions of Keonjhar and Dhenkanal constituting about twenty three percentage of state's population, beside the Saoros,

Kondha, Didayi and the little known Bondas. Each of these tribal communities has its own heritage of rituals, which are interesting anthropologically too. Mahapatra says,

> Orissan culture has been influenced to a considerable extent by the aboriginals, and it is common knowledge that folk and tribal elements are an integral part of Hindu ritual and living. It is believed that the original inhabitants of Orissa were such primitive tribes akin to the Saoros and Juangs, groups living in the wooded hinterland. Here, in the dense jungles, were ambiguous essences symbolised and made into ritual objects. Legends say that the original deity of the Saoros was a log of wood, which slowly became transformed into the image of Lord Jagannath – an indication that the origins of the cult of Jagannath lie in tribal totems. Even today a select group of priests of tribal origin are deputed to carry out certain tasks connected with the deity's worship...Totem and taboo are prevalent amongst the tribals... Magic forms an integral part of the tribal religion, and its practices are many... Here beats Orissa's primordial heart (*Orissa,* p.32-33).

Orissa abounds in temples. One can easily count five hundred temples in the old city of Bhubaneshwar alone – "An array of temples built systematically through the centuries, in chronological order form the sixth century to the thirteenth century AD"(18). The Jagannath temple at Puri, the Lingaraja temple at Bhubaneshwar and the Sun Temple at Konarka now in ruins, are the landmarks of Orissa and the living monuments of its highly developed, sophisticated temple sculpture and architecture. They symbolise man's quest into the realm of the unknown and stand, as mysterious as their presiding deities inside the dark sanctum sanctorum, where both illusion and reality become inseparable and indistinguishable. Hence temples are "a museum of symbols" (40) for anybody who cares to study them with perseverance and patience; and they point to an "unending rhythm"(16) in the flux of time – a journey towards infinity seeking to encompass eternity as an "ancient rite of dead years / makes its obeisance of life" (15). Therefore, temples and rituals constitute the hub of Orissa.

A sense of timelessness and spacelessness pervades the poetry of Jayanta Mahapatra. Orissa is the land where time seems to stand still, without moving in the direction of change. "We watch time-bound people go through their daily routine in the same unhurried way that their ancestors have done for centuries"(19). For example, on a pleasant October morning we shall not miss the familiar sight of Gobinda Maharana, the image maker, deeply engrossed in making the clay image of Durga ("from clay / the goddesses take their sacred shapes / in every autumn." p.34) to be worshipped during the festival of Durga Puja: a veneration of the Female Principle as Mother Goddess. Mahapatra observes Gobinda Maharana walking down the road to the club-house in Cuttack where he moulds the ten-armed, life-size clay image of Durga in her dual role as Creator and destroyer, with reverence, passion and humility in the same unchanging traditional way of his ancestors.

> Like his father before him, and his father's father, Gobinda stolidly pursues his ancient craft, and I cannot but notice a certain inner impulse which drives him on, part poetic, part divine. I look up at the images... Slowly I realise that I am living at one particular instant in many layers of time – the mythic, the historical and the present; and what I see in the present is only what has stirred the air of countless generations (36).

Even the ritual of *Cherapahanra* has an interesting point for consideration. In the traditional ritual of *Cherapahanra*, the King of Puri is called on to perform the duty of a sweeper before the deities at the time of the yearly chariot festival – an act of utter humility and submission to the Will of the Lord, which is continued to this day both in action and spirit. During the annual Car Festival, when the deities are installed ceremoniously in the chariots, "Raja of Puri sweeps the platforms of the chariots in the manner of his ancestor, King Purusottama, eight hundred years ago"(26). Only then the Lord starts on his symbolic tour of the Universe to study the fate of mankind, in the massive wooden chariot, accompanied by his brother Balabhadra and sister Subhadra, in only slightly smaller but nevertheless gigantic chariot. ("The giant chariot jostles like a toy / in a million hands." p.32). Here, Mahapatra compares the "giant chariot" to a tiny "toy". Chariot represents godliness and divinity whereas toy stands for playful childhood coupled with irresponsibility. By juxtaposing these two, Mahapatra demonstrates his ambivalent attitude to the famous *Ratha Jatra* the symbolic tour of Lord Jagannath – which is held every year in the month of July amidst great rituals and pomp. Mahapatra says that:

> Temple chronicles specify a height of 45 feet for Jagannatha's car, with 16 wheels, each 7 feet in diameter. Deep yellow and red colours characterise this car. Balabhadra's car, slightly smaller, is 44 feet in height and has 12 wheels, each with a diameter of 6 feet. It is covered in red and blue. Subhadra's car is crimson, 43 feet high, and sports 12 wheels of 5 feet diameter each (25-26).

These minute details of the rituals, both in their form and content, are yet another manifestation of frozen Time (Sun Temple at Konarka) is built so magnificently in the form of an immense stone chariot which stands on the three-metre-wide twenty four stone wheels (symbolising the hours of a day) being pulled by seven horses (symbolising seven days of a week) shown in the action of pulling the giant chariot through its course in the high sky which infact symbolises constant motion. But the life-style in Orissa has hardly moved away from its time honoured, traditional ways. Therefore, we have reasons to believe that all these ritualistic practices, perhaps, will be continued uninterrupted and unchanged into the future, the way they used to be in the distant past, because "Oriyas have always stuck to their own ways" (12) of living and the agriculture-based rural Orissa is a classic example of permanence and changelessness.

> Oriyas are reluctant to leave the village... the land is, to all accounts, their mother – however hungry he is, (the Oriya farmer) will not leave his home and the special bit of earth that has absorbed the ashes of his fathers (9-10).

All beliefs, customs and rituals connected with agriculture in a predominantly agrarian society of the rural Orissa still survive with the grandeur of antiquity. Therefore, Mahapatra feels that Time has had no impact on the ways Oriyas have been living their lives, i.e., the passage of time. Here, Mahapatra communicates how the rituals and traditions are inherited defying the passage of Time and how they still exert their strong influence on our ways of living especially in Orissa. Thus, countless generation of Oriyas have lived the same way facing similar ordeals and in the whole chain of endless movements, sons have merely replaced fathers. Mahapatra's sense of timelessness and spacelessness lies precisely in the fossilised life-styles and the antiquated attitudes of his people living in the predominantly rural landscape of Orissa.

Perhaps this is the main reason why even to this day, Orissa still remains one of the least developed Indian states. Orissa's sprawling backwardness is as well known as its magnificent, many –splendoured cultural history! The former is deplorable and the latter highly adorable and admirable!

Lord Jagannatha reigns supreme in Orissa, rather in the hearts of every devout Hindu. Our understanding of Orissa, and the poetry of Mahapatra, would never be complete without our knowing the cult of Jagannatha. Vasant. A. Shahane too feels that

> Jagannath Puri has assumed the position of a central character in several of Jayanta Mahapatra's poems – it is, as it were, the central consciousness of the poet's creativity which flows into the making of these poems.[4]

Mahapatra, on entering the sanctum of the Puri temple, feels that

> The three gods (Lord Jagannatha, his elder brother Balbhadra and sister Subhadra), darker than the darkness, strange, limbless, grotesque, the stark round eyes seeming to move darkly, circling and drawing me with the rope of my breath into a land where I stand, transfixed, repeating to myself: 'Do what you want. I am ready. Join my life' (28).

Lord Jagannatha is "strange, limbless and grotesque" which makes the reader realise that Mahapatra cannot respond to the image of the Lord as the Supreme One. At the same time, Mahapatra is drawn to it "with the ropes of my breath" as if he moves towards the image against his own wishes driven by an inner compulsion and he submits his free will to the Will of the Lord as if in a trance. Mahapatra's divided inheritance – his grandfather's conversion to Christianity and his own Hindu roots – results in such a complex ambivalence as seen throughout Mahapatra's poetry and prose writings. Legend has it that Raja Indradyumna performed *Ashwamedha Yaga* and the Lord, being pleased, granted to appear to him as a log of wood with special characteristic marks, floating down the Mahanadi. None of the King's sculptors could carve the image of Lord Jagannatha out of the log of wood, as their tools broke everytime they attempted. Finally, an old carpenter, Ananta Maharana (believed to be God himself in disguise), assured the King that he would complete the task provided the King agreed to lock him for 21 days and the temple doors be opened only after the stipulated date. The King agreed. But the queen had doubts about the old carpenter's skills and prevailed upon the King to open the temple doors before the appointed time. To their great surprise, they saw three incomplete shapes without limbs and hands. And that is how the Jagannatha – Trio came to be worshipped. Mahapatra says,

> Perhaps nowhere else in India are deities worshipped in such unfinished, in conceivable forms as in the temple of Jagannatha at Puri. The common Oriya believes in the Supremacy of Lord Jagannatha; for even though he has no arms or legs, his reach encompasses every corner of the world (26).

In his *Relationship*, Mahapatra alludes to the ritualistic practice of replacing the sacred deity of Lord Jagannatha, along with Balbhadra and Subhadra, at the Puri temple at a festival called the *Navakalevara* (the new body) which is observed once in twelve years. The new images of the deities are carved from the *neem* trees found in "the dense jungles" of Orissa, and then the "wood becomes a conceiver of life"(11) as it is transformed into the images of the presiding deities ready to be worshipped by the devotees. Mahapatra explains the elaborate rituals prescribed for the *Navakalevara*.

Chosen temple attendants are sent into the deep Orissa forests to search out certain neem (margosa) trees, marked by prescribed signs, and bring them back to the temple. There the tree trunks are carved into new forms identical to the old ones. When the images are complete, a specially chosen priest is blindfolded and led into the sanctum. The doors are then closed. The priest next takes the soul (unidentified relic) from the sealed body of the old image, rewraps it in leaf and seals it in the body of the new image, which is then placed on the altar to be worshipped. This is partly religious ritual, partly a way of life for thousands of Oriyas who value permanence and changelessness in their day-to-day existence (27).

This quotation offers an explanation to the concept of Navakalevara which in fact reads as a commentary on the preceding quotation.

However, it is important to note that Mahapatra does not gloat over the glories of Lord Jagannatha, nor is he concerned with the temple rituals or its spiritual implications or the mystery of the cult of Jagannatha in absolute terms. Infact, the poet in Mahapatra is guided by a different logic – "the need to be human is important in a poet than in anyone else": therefore, the guiding force of the poetry is a pervading sense of involvement and a humanitarian concern for the welfare of his people. When Mahapatra sees stark poverty around him and the starving children crying for the slices of watermelon on a hot summer afternoon, Mahapatra becomes indignant about the divine indifference of Lord Jagannatha, who becomes virtually the dead wood He is made of, because of His inability to alleviate hunger and suffering even in His own land. Orissa is also known as *Jagannatha Desa*: literally, the land of Lord Jagannatha. In "A Summer Afternoon", Mahapatra scoffs at "the atrocious innocence of Jagannath" who turns a blind eye to all the sufferings, especially of the children.

> Outside in the bright sun,
> the screams of five children crying for slices
> of watermelon pierce his ears:
> he sees a tree of ten hands
> scoffing the atrocious innocence of Jagannath
> in his sheltered shrine (40).

Where is compassion in His Round Eyes? Could He

be blind? Mahapatra wonders whether those are "fake huge eyes"(33) because they look vacantly without seeing. This shows that at least Mahapatra is not blind to the social realities. He does not deceive himself with an easy excuse of *Fate* or *Karma* to ease his conscience allowing his people to suffer. Mahapatra scoffs at the Lord in the face as it were, moved deeply by the sad plight of the children in whom he sees "a tree of ten hands"- a mocking reference to the ritual of carving the image of the Lord out of a *neem* tree. Unlike His image, these children are fully formed and their hunger is as real as the blood flowing in their weak bodies. Limbless, shapeless and grotesque as He is, how will He understand the needs of those who feel the hunger in the pits of their stomachs? Then it is a myth that His compassion reaches all, without discrimination and without prejudice. Mahapatra's poetic self refuses to accept such a grotesque Being as the saviour of mankind and as a redeemer of human miseries. Mahapatra reveals his stand as follows:

> Around me was sickness and hunger, the sufferings of people from malnutrition and disease – terrible form of disorder of the universe that made me question myself on the goodness of God we had been taught to believe in. And so I felt unable to reconcile these two affirmations – that God is the sum of all perfection, and that the world of ours, with all its imperfections was created by Him.[5]

This seems to be Mahapatra's intellectual response and the preceding one inviting the Lord to join his life, contradicting the rationalist in Mahapatra, seems to be born out of a mystical mood. Thus, the mystic, the poet, and the rationalist exist in Mahapatra's work. Therefore, it is not at all surprising to see such basic contradictions in Mahapatra's thinking as well as in his poetry. Mahapatra believes that *feeling* is central to a poem and the truth of a poem is independent of the poet's personal faith.

Today, somehow I have come to believe that the poet is neither a philosopher nor a logical being. Nor is he able to connect the value of a poem with the truth of what the poem states. It is feeling alone which seems to me the heart of the poem, and it is feeling which starts the poem in the mind of the poet. And perhaps, it is when the act of writing of the poem continues in the poet's mind that the poet truly learns to feel, moved by feelings itself, eventually being startled by it and experiences the expense of his art – before he gets his sense of life across.[6]

The above statement confirms the famous dictum that the poet as a creator is different from the man who suffers. Mahapatra's poetic search throughout has been an encounter with the other *within* and to come to terms with this "stranger within" him.

Poetry is the stranger within oneself – the man inside one is unaware of, and the poet is almost always in the quest of finding this other one. In this unending process of writing poetry, one is always trying to recognize oneself, finding out ultimately which part of oneself will finally outlast the other part.[7]

And this exploratory path is riddled with contradictions. Hence, to understand Mahapatra's writings, we should concentrate more on such contradictory statements or points of view, that search for a unified vision, which Mahapatra emphatically dismisses as utopian in the context of present day living.

The common problem of ambiguity and opacity encountered in the poetry of Mahapatra, infact, has its roots either in the incidents of his personal life or in the ritualistic life-style of his people in Orissa grounded in the mysteries of the remote past. Therefore, an acquaintance with both these factors not only helps us to place the experience of the poem in its proper context, but also becomes an essential prerequisite for our evaluative appreciation of Mahapatra's poetry. We may recall here Mahapatra's assertive stand on this point:

> How many people are aware of Orissa, historically, socially?...Therefore one's reading of my poem is bound to suffer – suffer in the sense that the poem will not give itself up fully to the reader if the reader isn't aware of the way we live in Orissa.[8]

Therefore, we may certainly feel handicapped if we lack the knowledge of both his life and the history of Orissa. In *False Start*, we can trace references to the *meria* (human sacrifice) practice that has been mentioned earlier. If we have no knowledge of this *meria* ritual, many of the poems would remain outside the periphery of our shared experience. Even those who summarily reject the autobiographical and historical approach as extraneous will see how they become mandatory in Mahapatra's poetry. Mahapatra himself states:

> A poet is, perhaps, only right when he says in his poem what he has actually known... Usually writers do rely on their individual personal experiences on those things that can be seen and heard, touched and trapped by their senses, which threaten their ephemeral existence – to produce their own poems. For, it is then that the poem becomes the only reliable authority to which one can turn to if one is to recognize the shapes of verse... A good number of my poems have their roots in day-to-day common experiences (10).

Meria – ritual, which was till recently prevalent among the Khonds of Phulbani – an ancient tribe of Orissa – is rooted in agricultural magic and the fertility cult of the primitive agrarian society. *Meria* is the human *sacrificial lamb* who is bought and reared with care and affection in the house of the tribal headman (*Saonto*). So, symbolically *meria* becomes the son of *Saonto*. On the auspicious day, with the priest's invocation and chanting of *mantras*, *meria* is sacrificed for the welfare and prosperity of the entire tribe. It is interesting to note that the first stab comes from the *Saonto* and the rest of the tribesmen fall upon the *meria* tearing him into bits, singing songs for peace and welfare. The tribal song rendered into English by Mahapatra reads as follows:

> Now we sacrifice the *meria*...
> Let there be abundant rains...
> And no famine strike the village.
> Let onions and garlic grow well
> And goats and cattle return home
> We merely feed the gods and Dhartani
> We have no guilt, we commit no crime
> We only offer the small sacrifice
> Too small for the gods, too small for the goddess
> Let them be pleased, let them make us happy (34).

The title of Mahapatra's poem "Time drawing In" suggests that the hour of the sacrifice is approaching fast. It also echoes the finality of the *Hour* and the *Deed* emphatically. There is a feeling that the mysterious hands of *Death* are gradually tightening their powerful grip around the slender neck of the meek *sacrificial lamb.* Of course, in the modern times, we do not conduct human sacrifices; the poetic recreation of this ritual is neither exact nor accurate because Mahapatra does not intend to faithfully record a *meria* sacrifice – that would be the job of a historian or anthropologist! Rather, Mahapatra wants to show how the edifice of a modern society is built on the terror of unsanctified blood as against the sacrificial blood of the primitive society and the modern *meria* is none other than the poet himself. The poem opens "In this December fog", which sets the scene for the mysterious rite. "Fog" denies us a clearer vision and whatever takes place in the foggy atmosphere is relevant only to this secret world.

In this December fog that comes crowding in
from nowhere, my life feels its weakness again,
and my secret nerves and blood leave me
with the mask of pain,
as the cool air of the humble leaves
hears the cry of the slaughtered sheep in the butcher-
house
and awakes;
my face proceeds bravely to drown
the fresh, taunting laughter that fills the hollow ears:
the grey water of doubt that will not wet
the throats of earth or sky (34).

The poet hears the fearful cry of the *meria* (himself) in the image of "a slaughtered sheep in the butcher-house".

> Cf: the mournful bleating of goats as they are led to the municipal slaughterhouse in my own town every morning awakes me (149).

> *Meria* – ritual is conducted for the benefit of the entire tribe whereas goats / sheep are slaughtered for satisfying the hungry. The sharp contrast in the purposes behind the two kinds of *sacrifices* is evidently self-explanatory! A comparison between the tribal song and its modern counterpart becomes inevitable and the inference, obviously, is too glaring! *Meria* sacrifice is sanctified by the noble purpose of appeasing the gods for the peace and prosperity of the whole tribe; the poet mock-seriously attempts to elevate the slaughtering of a sheep to the level of *sacrifice*, obviously on the implicit suggestion that the butcher caters to the twin demands of hunger and taste of a wider community! Therefore, the doubt as to whether or not such an act of *sacrifice* is essential or barbaric is irrelevant from the point of view of those who propitiate it, because they are solely guided by the welfare or the need of the respective communities

they think they are serving. The last two lines of the stanza quoted above justify this interpretation.

> Time draws in timidly
>
> each weakness, each fear to clear focus;
> and as the sun dulls the gleaming marigold in the fields,
> as the stones spread their designs over the hills
> and teach them the silent alphabet of belief,
> as the rain wears the mute, sightless seedout,
> I take the meat and bone of my body
> and lay this offering at the foot of the starless sky (34).

In contrast to the two types of sacrifices discussed earlier, when the poet becomes the *meria* taking out the meat and bone of his body as a sacrificial offerings, the ritual magic does not work any longer; instead, Nature turns inhospitable and hostile. Life energies are suppressed ("sun dulls the gleaming marigold in the fields") and there is no trace of fertility anywhere near in sight – "rain wears the mute, sightless seedout". Earth no longer guards the seeds in its womb to be grown into bountiful harvests, and the rain instead of nourishing the seeds, washes them out of earth's womb. The intended regenerative force proves abortive: the resultant "weakness and fear" counter the much desired pulsating, vibrant optimism. The poet feels utterly lost because his *sacrifice* has had no desired effect. He is condemned to be "haunted forever by loss" (36). There, is no rejoicing instead of resounding with the beating of drums and joyous laughter that follows a ritualistic sacrifice.

The modern *meria's* highly individualistic approach to life negates the very concept of a ritualistic sacrifice by robbing it of its conventional purpose and meaning. Nevertheless, the poet still nurses an intense longing to be an integral part of the society and to establish vital links with it while still retaining his individual identity. And the poet's anticipated joy at the very thought of all these becoming true almost like a miracle, and he waits with hope for that dawn to break in, dispersing the misty December fog.

Mahapatra, as we know was brought up as a Christian by his parents, especially the mother, who imposed a stern discipline on the growing child. But the atmosphere outside home was redundant with Hindu rites and festivals. Mahapatra experienced the pull of two religions in his early childhood, which left a permanent scar on his personality. Mahapatra was more and more drawn into an orbit of Hindu world view which has a dominant presence in the lives of the majority of our countrymen. Mahapatra admits that "Today my brother is a faithful Christian, a leader of the local community. I am not " (142).

It is of course wrong to assume that Mahapatra has embraced Hinduism. He is not interested in such simple solutions nor does he advocate it as a cheap prescription for a psycho-religious crisis. We must understand Mahapatra's genuine concerns for the world his grandfather was compelled to forsake by historical necessity.

> My grandfather, almost starving to death, has become a Christian century ago, quitting the Hindu fold when a devastating famine struck Orissa and people died by the hundreds, to be devoured by vultures and jackals. Shadows began to haunt me – of those voices that were no longer there, of a past that my father and mother made me forget. I was left alone, with my own insecure feelings, in an *akasa* that is there within the heart. I was left alone with my own moral uncertainty (151).

This uncertainty, as we have already seen, is central to Mahapatra's creativity. It is a fact that Mahapatra has his lineage deeply rooted in the Hindu culture and its ethos, from which he was estranged by circumstances: yet he experiences its pull as irresistible and real. However, Mahapatra believes that one should draw strength form one's own inner resources; the intrinsic quality of humanness should guide us in life more than any dogmatic beliefs. In the formulation of this conviction, Mahapatra acknowledges his debt to *Jean Barois*, a fiction by French novelist Roger Martin du Gard, which had a profound impact on Mahapatra because it taught him to rely on himself, to be true to his inner voice and to see that world as it really is.

Jayanta Mahapatra skillfully makes use of myths to give a wider appeal and a cosmic touch to the eternal problems of mankind, by moulding the mythological symbols into new forms and placing them in contemporary context. Myths operate at two levels – social and cultural – in Mahapatra's poetry. At either level, myths undergo a metamorphosis to bring into focus the present degradation and debasement of human life and its consequent loss of enduring quality. In the modern context, myths are stripped bare and they serve as poor travesty of their original rich symbolic suggestiveness. Hence, we experience the deglorification and sometimes even the debunking of myths in Mahapatra's poetry, which trait he largely shares with Keki. N. Daruwalla. For example, in Daruwalla's *Crossing of the Rivers*, the Ganges, the most sacred river of India, is realistically depicted as polluted because of the indiscriminate emptying of industrial waste into it, which has turned the Ganges into "swer-mouth"(11). The half-burnt corpses that float in the holy river make a horrible sight. Hence,

> The Ganga flows through the land,
> not to lighten the misery
> but to show it (16).

That the Ganga is believed to wash away the sins of people and thus purify them, while it always remains unsullied, is only a myth, becausc now the Ganges itself has become impure and defiled for all to see. Similarly, in Mahapatra, the Ganga is no more a spiritual purifier. The last rites to the dead performed on the banks of the Ganga, the ever burning funeral pyres at the ghats and the devout Hindu's last wish to disperse his *asthi* (bones and ashes) after his death in the holy Ganges – all these for Mahapatra, become "decorations" to the Ganges: and its banks are shrouded by mysterious rites and chanting of *mantras* directing and guiding the souls in their ascendancy to heaven. In "Our Imprecation, " Mahapatra alludes to this.

> The mouth is empty.
> Yet there is the River
> it catches, unaware:
> a Ganga
> decorated with histories of ashes
> like a mist of enchantments[9]

Mahapatra deftly turns the ashes of the dead into "histories of ashes", which suggests the individual history of every dead person and also the diverse histories of countless generations which paid their homage to the Ganga in the belief of cleansing their sins for attaining salvation are discounted by the decisive verb "decorated" and cures the reader as well as the poet of any illusion regarding the Ganga's mythical powers or significance in the present day.

> The Ganga stretches out its leisured hand,
> the whole of its vanity lying like an old newspaper
> that contains the poverty of those words which carry
> their own death with them. (34).

Again in "Our Imprecation", Kali, the mother-goddess appears in her fierce and ferocious incarnation as Kali; who throws out the destructive "Lava of horror"(8). Her "mouth" is "ulcered", an indication that the bleeding, lacerating wound will consume human civilisation at large like wild fire. Kali is set out to destroy not only the Evil which She is believed to accomplish, but indiscriminately everything as She herself is diseased in the mouth. As a result chaos, lawlessness and a terrible destruction is let loose on mankind; man has lost his capacity to love and even his dream is a "loveless museum"(9) and at the end, driven by "cosmic greed" (9) man also turns violent against his own kind "making only better murderers than lovers" (9) thus aiding his goddess in Her mission of reckless destruction. If Kali is subject to "ulcers" in the mouth, man cannot escape a similar plight, which visits him almost with a vengeance, striking a death-blow by sucking away all love from man's world leaving him,

> Quivering in
> the huge hunger of India
> That floods mouth with cosmic greed (9).

The "mouth"[10] is a recurrent image: it is the mouth from which the Ganga emerges and the Lava of horror erupts. The insatiable greed of man and his many "hungers" show through the gaping "mouth to the disgust of all, which "takes the fateful turn"(8), plunging man in perpetual misery and sickness of heart and mind. The mythical mouth of Child-Krishna in which Yashoda was shown *Brahmanda* (The Cosmos) resulting in a wondrous mystical experience of *self* and *Him*, remains perhaps "merely one dream"(9). Similar image is seen in the poem "A Dark Wind".

> India, like the decapitated old temple by the
> river, its mouth open, and starting,
> all its bewildering hunger born into
> sorrow (7).

The divine power – Kali – appears not as Protector

but as Destroyer – the Kali "playing with garland / of served heads / her girdle of severed hands" (54) and outstretched tongue conforms to "a predetermined pattern / of hunter and hunted"(32). The Creator has turned the Destroyer and the hunting spree will go on without respite. Hence, there is no rejoicing in the mythic past which has lost its magic, and the essence is replaced by superficiality. Human society has turned into "a rabid civilisation" losing itself in meaningless observation of rituals devoid of any significance or meaning, which sucks peoples' life-spirit away leaving them drained and exhausted (22). In *A Rain of Rites*, Goddess Durga herself has become one such dead-weigh bringing no benediction. During the festival of Durga Puja, people carry the clay image of the goddess more by habit than unstinted devotion, to the accompaniment of drummers "hammering on the deep stillness of the valley"(26).

> The ten-armed clay Durga
> framed in a mythic past,
> carried slowly twenty-four tired men (26).

"Hammering" indicates man's inner restlessness and his desperate need to break the monotony of boredom even at the cost of disturbing the serene quietness of the valley, producing a terrible numbness of senses. So both at the cultural and social level, myth has ceased to be functional in the traditional way. Hence, the contemporary reality now defeats the age old beliefs and practices. Over a period of time, the defilement of what was sacred and derangement of what was natural has come to be accepted complacently without producing any qualms in man's consciousness. In *Svayamvara* and *Other Poems*, Mahapatra depicts this deplorable situation with the calm acceptance of a man who is resigned to his fate.

Mahapatra shatters the mythic image of India through his realistic portrayal of our society in its stark nakedness. He also stresses how we have come to sympathise with the deviants and how tacitly we approve of, even perhaps appreciate, their ways. The ability to discriminate between right and wrong seems to be inoperative. Hence our loss is indeed too great. We have become powerless, silent spectators of "the disrobing of human values," weakened by the absence of moral righteousness, unable to draw sustenance from age – old myths (22). The poet holds himself answerable to the unpardonable apathy to the human suffering and deprivation for which, at one time or the other, we are all direct but mute witnesses; worse still, "we have fallen asleep / to the groans of the women taken in rape"(54). Nothing moves us, not even death, as we have become desensitised in the process of living our self-centred lives:

> Even in this remote, slack and wrinkled village
> on the bank of the Kaveri, the breeze
> trembles to the last breath of a drowned girl,
> Yet you move about, Jayanta,
> as though nothing had ever happened here.
> It is not as if anyone has to answer for it;
> I sit on the river bank wanting to smile
> for the destitute children who hang around the temple
> using their young years to shoo away the flies
> aroused by luncheon leftovers from city picnicers
> (24).

Here, Mahapatra confronts his poetic self to own his moral responsibility for the misery of "drowned girl". And the voice of his conscience seems to chide him for moving about "as though nothing had ever happened here". Mahapatra knows the bitter truth that endurance of suffering in the daily struggle for survival and existence renders anyone selfish, insensitive and callous to the needs of other fellow human beings. This dehumanising effect of poverty, hunger and deprivation is indeed deplorable. There seems to be no hope even for the "future generation" to restore dignity to the human person as the children have become "destitutes" and turned beggars and they "hang around the temple" in the hope of getting some food but sadly what they are destined for is only "luncheon leftovers from city picnicers". Even to claim this, the children have to "shoo away the flies"!

Jayanta Mahapatra's poetry makes exacting demands on reader response by creating dream-layers of experience where "the real and imagined calmly coalesce"; making our effort to distinguish the one from the other highly difficult if not impossible (18). Therefore, Mahapatra does not dare to disturb the mystery of myth born of the grand fruition of reality and imagination. He also perhaps feels that any attempt to unravel the mystery of myth would render it powerless. Hence, in "Myth" Mahapatra confesses that,

> I dare not go
> into the dark, dark sanctum
> where the myth shifts
> swiftly from hand to hand, eye to eye (22).

It may perhaps be true that what is real is too shocking to the senses, baffling to the eyes and aesthetically distasteful. Therefore, Mahapatra's poetic world, even when it depicts reality, doesn't show mirror-reflections; instead are exposed to a broad colour spectrum of over lapping images and symbols.

In his long-poem *Relationship*, Mahapatra deals with the Myth of Origin, i.e., myth of origin of this Universe and the myth of origin of man on this planet. Howsoever intelligent or advanced man may be in his thinking and technological accomplishments, his efforts in unraveling the Myth of Origin have at best remained only conjectural. There exists a series of missing links in the experimental verifications of the multiple hypotheses man has put forward. But the crux of the matter lies in the fact that while a scientist may be interested in the scientifically demonstrable aspect of the issue, poets have been equally concerned with the philosophical implications of such a quest and their relevance to man's life. Man has been eternally confronted with such question, as *Who am I? Where have I come from and where am I going to?* Continuing the same line of self-introspection, Mahapatra says,

> I ask myself: What am I made of? Of hunger and earth and home-sickness? Of loneliness and barbarism and the surprises of death? Yet I realise I cannot help being affected by the world around me, by a sensitivity to issues that plague my country and the whole world today. And in order to understand who I am and who I will become, I shall go on writing my poems.[11]

This persistent self-introspection is characteristic of Mahapatra's poetry which essentially remains exploratory in nature. Mahapatra is constantly haunted by questions that often seem to have no satisfactory answers, and Mahapatra's poetry reflects his almost obsessive preoccupations with a host of unanswerable questions. And Mahapatra succeeds in communicating the inevitability of our need to keep on asking questions about the problematics of life in order to come at least somewhere near the possibility of finding the most probable answers. Thus, one hopes that the explorations may lead one to a meaningful self-revelation. However, the answers or truths one arrives at, often remain highly personal, because, the validity and relevance of any answer or truth depends solely on the investigator's preferences, his mental preparedness, and finally, on the nature of his probings into the mysteries of life. A questioning attitude as against an uncritical passive acceptance and complacency, is basic to all serious and genuine pursuits. Therefore, a sensitive poet like Mahapatra frequently uses the *question form* in his writings. Commenting on this, Pushpinder Syal observes:

> A clear evidence of Mahapatra's exploratory technique,

> the series of 'questions' in the structure of a poem mark the progress of poetic explorations of a theme. They convey the puzzlement, the sense of wonder, indecision, groping in the dark and all the dilemmas of a conscience struggling with itself and the intransigence of life. Often the whole sequence of a poem is interspersed with questions. Beginning with a question, the poem proceeds in a crisis-cross of interrogations while this conveys an intensity of mental activity, it also gives the feeling of moving in a circle, condemned to wondering in a maze, without the possibility of relief.

Questions in Mahapatra's poetry occur much more frequently and consistently than in other poets, and serve the purpose of recapitulating moments of stillness and introspection. It is in the form of these quizzical interrogations that the silence, absences, doubts and fears that abound in the poems, grow on the reader with quiet but urgent insistence.[12]

While Mahapatra is no doubt concerned with the philosophical implications of such quests, he is equally attached to this world and not lost in reverie of metaphysical abstractions. Mahapatra anchors his quests firmly on the realities of this life. Even when he knows that the very nature of such probing will always remain inconclusive and unsatisfactory, a dialogue with it in the hope of getting atleast a glimpse of the truth. Therefore, Mahapatra explorations into the myth of origin do not lead him to the biblical parallel of Adam and Eve. Instead it is rooted in the non-Vedic derivative of Indian culture in the form of Tantrism with its supreme emphasis on *Prakriti* or the Female Principle. The union of *Prakriti* with *Purusha* or the Male Principle brings forth Cosmic creation in its entirely. It was believed by the *Tantrikas* (Practitioners of Tantrism) that cosmogony had a close parallel in human procreative principle. In the mystery of cosmogony because they believed that both the Universe and the human body are the expressions of the same principles and are composed of the same materials: *Panchabhutas – Bhoomiraponalonilonabhaha*, i.e., Five Element~ = Earth, Water, Fire, Air, Space. Even the etymology of the word Tantra lays emphasis on the act of procreation so predominantly associated with Tantrism, the origin of which has been traced back to the agricultural magic and fertility cult. Since, Orissa being primarily an agrarian society, it is only natural that any cult connected with agriculture and fertility should triumph and Mahapatra utilizes the suggestive power of this cult to celebrate life-forces.

In *Relationship* Mahapatra holds the *Deha Tattva* in high esteem.

> This is the real body: raging pachyderm
> with the crazy testicles, red and wild,
> the lusting god of the blackest Siva night:
> thus it is that it can hardly contain ourselves(27).

The Mukteswara temple (9th century AD), Parasurameshwara temple (7th century AD) and Vaitala temple (8th century AD) in Bhubaneshwar clearly show the rudiments of tantric cult. In the *Jaganmohana* (porch) of the Mukteswara temple, Mahapatra says, one can see the *Sapta Matrikas* (seven incarnations of the Mother Goddess as Brahmi, Maheshwari, Aindri, Kaumari, Vaisnavi, Varahi and Chamunda) and the figure of *Virabhadra* (born of Shiva) carved elegantly in the eight petals of a lotus – *astadalapadma* (20). Here is an unmistakable clue that this temple was once the centre of Tantric rites because in Tantrism lotus is a symbolic representation of the Female Principle. Similarly, in the Parasurameswara temple one can observe the sculptures of emaciated ascetics, their ribs showing plainly, engaged in the worship of *Linga* (20). And the "Vaitala temple dedicated to Chamunda, the fearful mother goddess. Here, about 1200 years ago, unimaginable Tantric rites were performed. An image of Siva in his most terrible form, sporting a garland of skulls, with a protruding tongue and hollowed belly, points to the influence of Tantrism on Saivism"(21).

When Orissa is so full of the impact of Tantrism, it is natural for Mahapatra to be highly influenced by the Tantric motifs. Mahapatra says that our Tantric ancestors' quests should not be dismissed as a perverted system of rites, because their *ideas* certainly paved the way for the development of scientific spirit of inquiry into the nature of things, which is indeed the "messianic gain of this new cult"(15). Thus, Mahapatra's ordering of myths acknowledges our debts to the experiments of our ancestors that led to the development of the human society, perpetually encouraging and enriching man's intellectual pursuits in the domain of materialistic outlook of life.

The most curious and significant feature to be observed in Mahapatra's poetic world is his inability to maintain relationship either with his wife Runu Mahapatra, whom he loved and married against stiff opposition from his parents, which eventually led Mahapatra to leave the house of his parents and set up his own home. Although, he confesses that "I have a flirting relationship with some girls."[13] But, after two decades of his marriage, when Mohan – his only son – left for studies, Mahapatra experienced a sudden void and he confesses that "the house was empty... And Runu lived almost in herself, although we shared the same house"(146). Hence Runu and Mahapatra were leading their own isolated lives, but despite the fact Mahapatra confesses that "I still love my wife."[13]

Although, Mahapatra's not-so-good relationship with his mother right from his childhood and Mahapatra never felt the warmth of maternal love and therefore the mother was always "A Missing Person." Mahapatra grew up almost as a lonely child in the house as his younger brother was born when Mahapatra was nearly four, and his sister first set her eyes on him nine years later. Mahapatra says,

> Perhaps my discontentment was in that there was no one in the house to talk to [. . .]. so often I longed for someone in whom I could confide, like a sister or a cousin of my age–but this didn't come about [. . .]. More than anything else, my reading took my mind away from the terrible discomfort I felt more and more in the house, as I tried to resist my mother's actions – those accusations of hers I knew were totally unjustified and merely impelled by her own ill-founded fears. I kept more and more to myself (138-140).

Therefore, the image of his mother, physically ill, moving about in the listless darkness of the house was deeply ingrained in Mahapatra's mind which found expression, thirty years later in 1970, in the poem titled "A Missing Person". The poem is quoted in full.

> In the darkened room
> a woman
> cannot find her reflection in the mirror
> waiting as usual
> at the edge of sleep
> In her hands she holds
> the oil lamp
> whose drunken yellow flames
> know where her lonely body hides (7).

This poem is rooted in Mahapatra's childhood, is one of those poems which transcend their real setting. Indian women are basically "missing persons", especially in the social settings of the rural Indian life, which moves at a snail's pace. She waits indefinitely to find her own reflection in the fulfilment of her womanhood beyond the conventional role of a wife and a mother. Mahapatra says,

> ... what the woman is waiting for, she has been waiting for years, for aeons, for ages. So, it's both set in a moment and set in time... And my poems are not urban poems, they are not set in cities like Bombay or Delhi. The life people lead is a life which has remained unchanged through decades, through centuries. And so there is a sense of tolerance, a sense of endurance. You couldn't call it apathy, you couldn't call it indifference, but one waits with a smile for the next life. I guess the poem suggests that (22-23).

Though Jayanta Mahapatra loved his father, his poetry depicts only an overpowering archetypal father figure and because of his basically shy nature, Mahapatra feels lonely wherever he goes and he finds it difficult to make friends. The effect of such experiences is perhaps responsible for the relational crises that we see in Mahapatra's poetry. Deserted by all, Mahapatra feels lost in the vast sea of unstable, sterile human relationships and shrinks with the thoughts of dying unmourned by his own family and friends, feeling separated and repelled by all human contacts.

> I can't remember hearing anyone
> saying he will mourn for me when I am gone (39).

Infact, the desolate ruins of Konarka sing a dirge on the loss of all human relationships in Mahapatra's poetic world. Hence, the only relationship that gets built up in the poem, volume after volume, is Mahapatra's relationship with his own self; and, in this sense, his poetry is a journey into the self.

REFERENCES

1. Righter, William. *Myth and Literature*. London: Routledge and Kegan Paul, 1975. 3.

2. Jung, Carl G., ed. "Approaching the Unconscious: The Analysis

of Dreams," *Man and His* Symbol. Carl G. Jung 1968; New York: Dell Publishing Co., Inc., 1973. 45.

3. Sivaramakrishna, M., ed. "Tongue in English Chains: Indo-English Poetry Today," *Indian Poetry in English: A Critical Assessment.* Vasant A. Shahane and M. Sivaramakrishna Delhi: Macmillan India Private Ltd., 1980. 11.

4. Shahane, Vasant A., ed. "The 'Naked Earth and Beyond': The Poetry of Jayanta Mahapatra", *Perspectives on Indian Poetry in English.* M.K. Naik. New Delhi: Abhinav Publication, 1984. 151.

5. Mahapatra, Jayanta. "Through the Looking Glass," *Times of India.* March 28 1992. 2.

6. Mahapatra, Jayanta. "The Voice in the Ink," *The Illustrated Weekly of India.* April 1, 1990. 28.

7. Mahapatra, Jayanta. *Indian Literature.* 150. 42.

8. Mahapatra, Jayanta. interview. Raja Rao. *Ten Indian Writers in Interview.* Calcutta: Writers Workshop, 1991. 20.

9. Mahapatra, Jayanta. "Our Imprecation," *Journal of Indian writing in English* 10.1-10.2 Jan-July 1982. 8.

10. Mahapatra, Jayanta. interview. Raja Rao. *Ten Indian Writers in Interview.* Calcutta: Writers Workshop, 1991. 22-23.

11. Mahapatra, Jayanta. *Indian Literature.* 150. 43.

12. Syal, Pushpinder. "The Use of Language," *The Poetry.* 205.

13. Mahapatra, Jayanta. In conversation with Rahul Mene. *UGC Sponsored National Seminar on "Indian Ethos in Indo Anglian Literature."* Durg: 21-22 Oct. 2005.

6

Growing Materialism and Corruption of Humanity

This chapter intends to record growing materialism and corruption of humanity on contemporary life and society as well. He feels agonised about real living of poor people. The poet's anguish is palpable as the life has gone astray with the jungle law. Mahapatra dwells on hunger, violence and terrorism. He judges political issues from the humanistic view point. He depicts the predicament of human life. Mahapatra tries in vain to speak out realities of life in India. He thus tries to identify himself with the complex problems of the society as a humanist.

As a modern poet Jayanta Mahapatra tries to 'connect' himself with the contemporary world and he realises that he should be "aware of what's going on around him: the poverty, the greed, the unnecessary violence, the cruelty, the injustice, the sexuality."[1] Man's cruelty to man has become the order of the day. Mahapatra lament such a situation in a poem called 'Dawn':

> Things are only going their way.
> The dawn appears headless again.
> The child has already come to know,
> from who knows whom
> that peace has gone, never to return. (62)

The poet's brio lies in exploiting the day-to-day situations out of the contemporary world. Life in India has drowned headlong in poverty, wretchedness and destitution in the poem "Unreal Country." The poet says that the heritage of our culture has waned over the centuries and it is understood to be at nadir because of self-centredness of the leaders of the country. Mahapatra portrays the country:

> Rain grates in the silence. My son
> walks in through the dim walls,
> a strange map drawn by life. (4)

Rain causes havoc to the silent, peaceful lives of the people. The young are consequently steeped in unemployment and are drifting along. The present scenario of the country smacks of their vitality and hope and has left them in the lurch. The position of the youth is thus "a strange map drawn by life."

The young men, depresses and dejected, deign themselves to resign to their lot. They feel like leading their adrift life in the shelter of night in which they feel secure and cosy on the other side of 'disappointment and despondency.' Mahapatra feels aghast at the disgruntled and dejected face of his son. His son feels as if the whole world has become desolate and deserted. Mahapatra comments on the contemporary life of India:

> His lost face, white enamel,
> looks down at his feet
> as if to say: Only the world
> is left, and the rain
> that hangs from the branches. (4)

The expression "His lost face, white enamel, looks down at his feet" echoes a line from *The Waste Land:*

> And each man fixed his eyes before his feet
>
> ("The Burial of the Dead," line 65)

Eliot speaks about spiritual degradation in the people of England. Mahapatra voices his concern about the 'waste land' of India fraught with hopelessness and despondency of the unemployed youth. He remarks that the 'rain' is a destructive force hanging like the sword of Damocles.

Mahapatra casts aspersions on the failure of the government to provide succour to the people in their need. The poet's father is the mouthpiece to vent the poet's feelings of vexation.

> And through the dull suburbs
> of his death, my old father
> gropes his way back.
> Yes, he seems to whisper,
> overwhelmed by the defeat
> in my eyes, hunger and earth
> made the bones of one's breath. (64)

'Hunger and earth' are connotative of famine and drought in 1866 when the poet's father underwent an excruciating suffering. Famine wreaked havoc on his family, and on the lives of the Oriya people in 1866. Natural calamities undermine common people. They remain miserably alive with skeletal life in them. The poet gives vent to his fury and agony at the callousness of the destructive 'rain' and 'heartlessness' of the leaders. He remarks:

> I see them nod to each other,
> suddenly in fear of the rain,
> of the heart left behind. (4)

The poet depicts India as a physically waste land. The very title of the poem is suggestive of both "reality in Unreal Country" and "unreality in real country." The first aspect suggests that as in Utopia everything appears to be orderly and truthful. The second one denotes unreality realized in the real country. It means the country is fraught with deceit, hopelessness, despair, despondency etc. which can be experienced in the real country.

These characteristics are due to hunger of which Mahapatra is ever conscious. He gives a befitting reply to the question of Kazuko Shiraishi, the scientist of Tokyo, in "A Letter of Kazuko Shiraishi" about the day-to-day problems faced by India. The poet says that most of the seven-hundred million Indians are hunger-stricken and die of starvation. He lays emphasis on hunger comparing it to 'rain.' Hunger smacks Indian masses:

> It's rain again. Going on and on all day.
> Like hunger. You would think this country
> has nothing but seven hundred million bellies (29)

It implies that rain batters the Indian landscape with its devastating floods and causes hunger. Mahapatra is a mute witness to devastation. He expresses diatribe against the leaders of democratic India who make profuse platitudes vociferously. He remarks:

> I am one of them, listening to the radio each day
> and learning more about fertilizers and democracy
> (29)

The leaders never think of stemming the outflow of rainy water into the seas, by building projects. Torrential rain inundates the lands causing havoc to the masses. Abortion has been legalised to arrest the growth-rate of population. The Government fails to provide sufficient medicines to hospitals. Deaths occur on account of delivery, septicemia etc. Recklessness of the Government becomes apparent as Mahapatra tells about the death of a thirteen year-old servant-girl.

> our thirteen-year-old servant-girl died last week
> of tetanus and I just kept waiting, even after
> the end. Waited without reason for the world's people
> to dream of that girl's future. (29)

The poet points out the failure and inability of the government to enact abolition of child-labour. He lashes out at the superstitions of the Indian masses. God did not come to the rescue of the servant girl despite her fating and vermilion on her throat. It implies the falsity of gods. Mahapatra interprets that when time comes, each man dies. And time 'eternal' alone remembers her in its continuum. He remarks:

time would remember how it emptied itself
into the hands of the young girl, and how that time
blew away softly with her (29)

Here, poet tries in vain to speak out realities of life in India. He thus tries to identify himself with the complex problems of the society as a humanist. It seems obvious when he deeply reacts to certain events. One such occasion is when he finds political leaders flamboyantly participating in celebration of inauguration of some new postage stamp as a token of anniversary of a great leader who is considered to have rendered laurel service to the country.

The poet chastises those leaders for their panache-appearance on the occasion while the country appears to be sterile with famished faces. He expresses his concern in Section 1 of "The Twenty-Fifth Anniversary of a Republic: 1975":

This is a barren world that has been
prowling round my room, epidemics in the poisoned air,
dusty streets stretching away like disgruntled socialists (17)

The world is steeped in abysmal poverty and nauseous epidemics. The trope "This is a barren world" echoes Eliot's lines in "The Hollow Men":

This is the dead land
This is the cactus land (Part III, 1-2 lines)

The hollow men's world is an unproductive land and it is spiritually dead. Mahapatra depicts the political leaders as lacking in real spirit for advancement of people. The world's atmosphere is wholly vitiated by sanguinary politics. It appears to the poet's that the streets have stretched far away before his eyes with the sprawling disappointment and nervousness like the disgruntled politicians despite their wealth and prosperity. Mahapatra condemns the politicians for their flamboyant ostentation.

> The new postage stamp gleams in silver and grey
> (17)

He lashes out at the insidious act of politicians who indulge in celebrating a great leader's birth anniversary by releasing a new postage stamp in his name.

Mahapatra opines that unless and until the lives of the poor are uplifted, the very act of releasing a new postage stamp is futile and otiose. He says:

> it's such a thing that brings a faint flush on our weeks,
> like a sudden wing that slips under the door and stirs
> the papers silent on the desk and other objects
> that have learnt to live without their knowing. (17)

The poet does not feel happy over such celebrations. He conjectures that even if the leaders do not think of performing such acts with new strategies to bring light in the lives of the poor, the poet himself and the masses would not feel deterred by continuance of poverty. The recalcitrant attitude of the poet surfaces with a question:

> Do we wait to feel the ground give way beneath us?
> (17)

The poet tries to put some pep into the poor people and says that they can fend for themselves. He thus tries to identify himself with the society.

Mahapatra condemns political leaders for their sham and hypocritical acts. The present-day politicians hoodwink the common people with intrigues. They stood down to the level of making a fetish of erecting statues of worthless leaders on the cross-roads. He expresses his views in Section III of "The Twenty-Fifth Anniversary of a Republic: 1975":

> There are new statues on the cross-roads, newer dead,
>
> that are visible from far and wide. (19)

The poet points out that in the past, only the statues of the great leaders who could sacrifice themselves for their lofty ideals were erected and such statues could be seen here and there in the big cities. Now-a-days, the statues are being installed on the names of the leaders who indulged in nefarious acts, crimes etc. the poet criticises the leaders who squander away the valuable coffers of the government and cause the despicable dead leaders to snowball into significance. He detests the leaders to make a fetish of some contemptuous leader.

Mahapatra expresses his anguish and angst about the degenerate values which have seeped into the contemporary life of the country. Self-centredness of people and leaders looms large in the nation's politics. Partisan outlook and debased moral values have despoiled the country of its image. The poet articulate unhappiness in "Another Love Poem." He remarks:

> Today I seek no reason for what
>
> has happened to me. Do I ask too much land? (63)

The poet dislikes to pore over the recounting of certain problems which tarnished the image of the country. He shall shoulder the responsibility of refurbishing the lost glorious image of India. The leaders and the citizens had better take upon themselves the task of rebuilding the image without subjective, lopsided view, and think with all the objectivity about amelioration of the country in all the facets. Mahapatra remarks with a hope:

This country lives, on its image (63)

Bijay Kumar Das comments, "He (the poet) is conscious of keeping the image of the country alive. In the international field our country should maintain impartiality and objectivity."[2] On the contrary, the old strife-riveted politics has thrown the country into a shambles. The poet voices his peevishness about the self-centred politics and policies. The lofty ideals set by the older generations have been thrown into limbo. The country is not in a position to retrieve its lost glory, as it seems to be drowned in frustration and lack of commitment towards the onward march of progress. The ugly scenario cannot be mitigated as the leaders have slacked off their efforts to rebuild the nation. The nation bewails them who have sapped and undermined it.

Mahapatra also portrays the whole ambience of violence and destruction. Each dawn begins with a nightmarish experience to men, women and children. The children are no exception to brutalities. "Violence upon the road" is apparently visible. Children dread to imagine that peace never returns, as the land is full of undulations owing to disorder and anarchy. Violence has spread in every nook and cranny except over the foothills. No protest against violence is noticed. The poet decries meaninglessness of silence – silence which is distinguishable from the silence of beatitude. He also denounces people who escape for fear of violence shedding their courage and bravery to fight terrorism. These cowards are living a life of silence. He condemns the escapists:

The foothills survive.
Footsteps of a few who walked on them
are silent.
Only grass, with ancient heavy feet
has stayed behind
in the frail shelter of that sound (62)

The poet says that the escapists are leading a very comfortable life which is in no way significant and worthwhile. According to him, the grass is trampled upon and yet it stands erect and survives withstanding all odds among the sounds of the footsteps of the escapists.

The poet is reminded about the brutal assassination of Smt. Indira Gandhi. Through image of violence and terrorism it shows the rapid degeneration that has crept into the veins of the country and the countrymen:

Pale light slashes the streets.
For a second I see Indira Gandhi
looking wistfully at her garden.
As I near the edge of the flowers,
I realise she's dead too. (57)

He could perceive the death of Indira Gandhi in his mental vision. He feels regretful about her sudden demise, recalling to his mind all the advancement in all facets she had made. But the young men reveled in their heroic deed under the wrong notion that they had slain her. The whole country remained stock-still on hearing the news of her death. The poet expresses thanks to her for progress of India. He remarks:

Perhaps all of India
is not awake at this hour.
Submerged in her immensity,
I know I too cannot get away. (57)
Mahapatra laments the death of Indira Gandhi:

Like a patient crocodile
she leaves her prey to rot into softness,
fastened beneath the roots
of some banyan of our heritage
that overhangs the river of our time. (58)

She believed in the gunmen, but they betrayed her. Though she was shrewd, she could not sense the forthcoming premonition and fell prey to the perfidy of the betrayers. She could pitch her roots into the cultural heritage of the country. Bijay Kumar Das comments, "The problems that bedevil us are being lost sight of. Indira Gandhi's sacrifice is too big to be understood at the moment."(60)

Mahapatra feels angst about inhuman and brutal murders occurring in the country, more especially in Punjab where terrorism and violence have sprawled awkwardly, and he reacts to such events or acts as he is struck by conscience. He delineates Punjab as a State chock-full of awful murders. Punjab is rocked by senseless movement of anti-national activities in the name of Khalistan. Bloodshed and violence have become the hallmark of Punjab. Death is an all-pervasive force. The poet expresses horror and shock in "Bewildered Wheatfields: Section 1":

A death lasts (14)

The poet grows immensely pathetic as Punjab, once impregnated with greenery of wheatfields has drifted into a land of bloodshed and violence. He rues:

The dry riverbed

Wrapped up in a shroud of moonlight (14)

Punjab, which brimmed with overflowing rivers once has now turned dry because of blood-thirsty killings. Moonlight also has been shrouded in inhumanity. He regrets:

This night of the decaying bodies
of those whom I love,
reverberates
with the ruined light of stars. (14)

People were murdered in broad daylight. It looked as if the day metamorphosed into the night. The word "reverberate" connotes how Punjab echoed with gruesome, awful killings.

Violence and killings have become rampant in Punjab. Mahapatra feels that humanity has lost its entity. He puts his views across in "Section 7: Bewildered Wheatfields":

Here
I do not know
what I am looking for (20)

The poet's search for humanitarian thinking goes unrewarded as it is getting corrupt. He wonders whether a humanitarian can be found there. He thinks that such a man may exist only in dream. He unequivocally says that humanism is conspicuous by absence.

To be human
is to see in a dream perhaps
the one who can never be seen (20)

Mahapatra feels grief stricken as terrorists are hired to perpetuate brutal killings of the innocent people. He voices his concern:

perhaps to hire out a tractor
to work the fields
or to hook the slippery little carp
which swim
among the muddy paddies (20)

Punjab is rife with carnage by terrorists on the name of Khalistan movement. The poet contrasts perpetual killing with the meandering waterfalls. The water courses in a winding way whereas the terrorists have lost patience to look humanoid. The water is distinguishable from the terrorists:

> Waterfalls squirm
> with their quality of patience,
> of timelessness. (20)

Mahapatra feels cosy and comfortable as he stays away from the terrorists. The extermination of the innocent people persists continuously:

> Rain falls heavy, hard as stones.
> I am so faraway from these falls. (20)

'Rain' symbolises destruction. Hailstorm kills a large number of humans and animals. The terrorists like the rain resort to killing many people. The poet feels indeterminate whether he is safe and cosy, or he should grieve over the human loss in Punjab. He looks bewildered:

> I chance pain and prayer,
> the simple pendulum,
> trying my utmost to replace
> the senseless refrain of hate
> by the amazement to be alive. (20)

It displays the poet's dichotomy. He desires to go to Punjab to mollify the terrorists by convincing them of sinful acts. At the same time he shudders by imagining that he may be killed. He feels rather inclined to pray to God to keep him alive, as also the people of Punjab, by annihilating hatred and violence deep-seated in their hearts.

Mahapatra's identifying himself with the problems of the society is so profound that he wouldn't help asking Mahatma Gandhi whether love for violence has been handed down to the posterity which is engulfed in hostility and antagonism. The poet addresses Gandhiji's in "Section 20: Bewildered Wheatfields":

> Ah love, let us be true
> about you, about freedom. Was everything you did,
> Gandhiji, only an act you put on for posterity?
> With India, barely worth raping? (34)

Mahapatra feels that the political leaders are the root-cause of all the social maladies and upheavals being perpetrated by the terrorists in Punjab, Assam and elsewhere. The people in Punjab are vexed with the abuse of humanity. The leaders infused antagonism in the people against the Indian government. Later it grew into terrorism from mere protests in the beginning. Terrorism is the offspring of politics and has become rampant. The hard-core leaders have hardly thought of the very existence of the common people. The people of Punjab are caught in the grip of panic. The poet points out that the terrorist activities rocked Punjab is all due to the political skullduggery of the leaders for the selfish ends. Mahapatra hopes that the myths of India enlighten people and mitigate terrorism, and also peace is restored in Punjab which is floundering about in terrorism.

Mahapatra also articulates his view of what use the separate Khalistan is when it is attained by terrorism. The poet appeals to the people to exterminate terrorism as it is rooted in blind faith. It is like a hyena causing immense harm to the innocents. B. K. Das remarks, "The anti-national activities in Punjab in the name of Khalistan and the Bhopal gas tragedy have sent shock waves throughout the country."[3]It was in Bhopal gas tragedy which claimed a heavy death toll of innocent men, women and children due to gas-leakage in the Union carbide factory.

Mahapatra bemoans degeneracy of social and moral values. It is clear when he says in "30th January 1982: A Story." The day 30th January refers to the death anniversary of Mahatma Gandhi. People in the contemporary society have jettisoned the ideal of non-violence which Gandhiji advocated. The poet laments the people's merciless act of butchering cows and goats. The loose, conversational tone of the poem symbolises the lack of seriousness about moral values.

> Another day. Like any other.
> The bleating goat on the butcher's block
> Quickened its large breath and stare wide-eyed. (26)

The poet's reaction and response are immediate. He says, "The mournful bleating of goats as they are led to the municipal slaughter-house in my town every morning awakes me."[4] He identifies himself with the bleating of goats and pours out agony of goats as if he felt agonised.

The slaughtering of goats and sheep is a common phenomenon except on the days of 'Second October' and 'Thirtieth January.' He says that people have become oblivious of the above two days. B. K. Das points out, "The poet lays bare the hypocrisy of our people who pay lip service to Mahatma Gandhi's cult of non-violence but do not practice it."[5] Mahapatra laments the failure and the lack of responsibility of the Department of Public Relations in imposing the prohibition for observance on the Mahatma's birth and death anniversaries. Besides, the way rich woman reacted against the blaring announcement of the Public Relation Department is in sharp contrast to the way her five- year-old girl wished to pour life into the doll. He remarks:

> The rich woman cursed the Government
> for waking her up so early when it was not fully light.
> Her five-year-old daughter cuddled
> the broken doll's head in her arms for she needed to fill her life (26)

The poet lays bare the evil nature of man. He could not shed hereditary characteristic and feels prone to killing animals or fellow-beings. The poet comments:

> The empty bedroom sank heavily onto one of the evil schemes
> which led through the long night into dawn.
> and,
> As the scent of new mango blossoms blew in
> with the morning breeze, restless
> with the heritage of blood. (26)

A contrast is brought out between good and evil persons. Good is interpreted through mangoes while evil is represented by humans as they inherit it. They feel restless until an evil is done.

Evil has a vital role to play in society. It was the root-cause of assassination of Mahatma Gandhi. All that he had done was to follow truth and non-violence. It was too "bitter" for others to follow the percepts. Mahapatra interprets that the steps Gandhi had adopted were hazardous to certain fanatics. They were not prepared to undergo trials which exacted their precious lives hence, the fanatics wreaked vengeance on Gandhi and he writhed under spasms of pain while he breathed his last. Although, Mahapatra admits his weakness that he cannot follow Gandhiji's footsteps rather he feels optimistic that myriad people might be born to right the wrong with non-violence and truth.

While trying to mythicise Gandhi, Mahapatra realises that one can be authentic as a writer or poet by going back to his / her roots. In his case, he wants to decolonise himself and his culture so that he can be original and authentic, as a poet. In trying 'to be himself', he found his poetry. Thus he writes:

> And the poem I found at last,
> already lost in the small of the heart,

just to push the deep, nameless breath
into the hysterics of history. (8)

As Gandhi has become a living legend for us. Even when people disagree with him or his principles, they are conscious of his presence. He has become a part of Indian Psyche. In a fitting tribute to Gandhi the poet acknowledges Gandhi's unseen presence amongst us, the Indian. He says,

In me
your body opens slowly
as if you have been bound tight all your life,
as if flesh could see
what the mind believes is true. (10)

Mahapatra's angst over violence preempting non-violence in the society. He bemoans terrorism stalking in Punjab and depicts how non-violence is on death-bed and is surviving on glucose displays the feeble structure of the society. The terrorist movement is spawned in liaison with the government. The poet throws a trenchant remark against the culpable government. Thus Mahapatra identifies himself with the poor, down-trodden who are victims of the rich people, the self-centred leaders and the terrorists.

Moreover, Mahapatra talks about the disintegration of our world in the inferno of hate. We wage wars against our own brothers in the name of serving religion, by spreading vilely the seeds of hatred and violence. In *Dispossessed Nests*, Mahapatra depicts an incident of a plane hijacked by a pro-Khalistan terrorist:

The terrorist who hijacked Flight 405
to Lahore even doled out milk and fruit
to children and the old. He was a mere
boy, they said, he even smiled,
shook hands and broke down in the end
when everything got over [. . .].

> May be
> there were women on the aircraft
> who fell in love with the captors.
> And the bullets didn't hurt too perhaps [. . .].
> The vermilion on the woman's forehead
> ripples in the dark. Her kid daughter wants
> her favourite hijacking anecdote narrated again
> to lull her to sleep. (21)

In this poem, Mahapatra seems to negate the feelings of fear, uncertainty, torture and the psychological trauma one commonly expects from any terrorist activities: The terrorist "was a mere boy" and he did not intend to hurt the passengers on board of Flight 405. The terrorist showed unusual concerns for the children and the old as he "doled out milk and fruit" to them. Here, Mahapatra seems to register the profound tragedy of people involved in terrorist and such other activities. They are human; they are lovable; they are even heroic. Unfortunately, they embraced a wrong *cause* and one can only feel deeply sad about such people. What is also unfortunate but common is that a terrorist turns a hero and even the children come to love and enjoy a terrorist's tale as their favourite bed-time story: "Her kid daughter wants / her favourite hijacking anecdote narrated again / to lull her to sleep".

Essential social values of peace, universal brotherhood, love, patriotism no longer evoke a positive response; anybody who proclaims to be the harbinger of such values is looked upon with suspicion. Religion has ceased to be cohesive force binding people together, and in its place religious intolerance, fanaticism and fundamentalism raise their ugly heads. What is shocking is that we have blindly come to passively accept these perversions as natural. We seems to be addicted to violence and hatred. Mahapatra grieves over man's distorted values and its impact on the younger generations which grows in the corrupt atmosphere of displaced loyalties and secessionist tendencies. In this chaotic situation bordering on anarchy, Mahapatra feels lost and helpless.

The inexplicable and ruthless violences and injustices of contemporary society has begun to worry the poet. Gone is the dreamy exploration of a poetic consciousness; *Shadow Space*, even more than *A Whiteness of Bone* strives to express and catch the anguish, the pity and the horror of events that have shaken the country in the last two decades of this century: the Bhopal gas tragedy, the Gulf war, the Bombay riots of 1994, the Kalahandi starvation death, technology creating its own share of injustices of ancient India that still live on. Indian women, and their position in traditional structures have been the subject of Mahapatra's poem from the earliest collection. The eighth poem in *Shadow Space* 'Widow' that break the poem into patterns of light and shadow to present the horrific spectacles of Hindu widow, who forced to give up all joy and lead a life of absolute austereness:

> Her eyes drift from light and fire
> And settle slowly on the darkness of her bones [. . .].
> Her skin breaks into fickle shadows
> that trail her to the corner of the little room
> where a stone icon stands, weary with vermilion
> in an exotic drapery of hopes [. . .]. (20)

There is the traditional violence on the one hand and the violence of a society that is increasingly callous and numb to injustices and grief on the other. A large number of poems deal with the contemporary issues with a nervous energy that sometimes succeeds in creating good poetry and sometimes fails quiet badly.

On August fifteenth every year the poet's wound deepens. Violence today has placed its grip on people. Today people have forgotten the sacrifices, for which India became free, the human pettiness and greed. Looking at the plight of Gandhiji's photograph:

> The photograph of Gandhiji's in the new airport lounge
> is more than forty years old.
> Every time I look into the oldman's eyes,
> he calmly hands my promise back to me.
> Land, our land,
> there is so much land between us now. (50)

Jr. martin C. Caroll has also claimed that the chief function of any genre of literature is "to reflect with meaning the totality of contemporary human conditions."[5] Jayanta Mahapatra's poetry is a reflection of social process. Naxalism is an Indian socio-political issue during the 1970's. In this context in the words of Asif Currimbhoy on the socio-political conditions of Calcutta during the Naxal period:

> The proximity of bloodthirsty violence rent the air, and before you knew it, it had pervaded the countryside, the classroom, the revolutionary, the intellectual, the deprived... and fear crept over the entire city... Indiscriminate killing followed, terrorist appeared under the guise of Maoist reform, and law and learning lay shattered...[6]

The violent young generation opts for the nefarious path of Naxalite violence. They feel that "the established order becomes an obstacle to progress."[7] Jayanta Mahapatra gives a vivid account of the Naxal movement:

> Why am I hurt still by the look
> in the hand of that graceful Naxal girl
> who appeared out of nowhere that winter,
> holding a knife as old as history? (29)

In "A Country," where "hunger keeps growing," a girl dies of starvation before her "breasts are swollen with milk" (29) and out of hunger a girl turns Naxalite. This poem is an attempt of the poet to come to grips with the prevalent spirit of his land that encompasses revolutions, protests and suffering. He realises much to his chagrin that the age-old myths are no answer to the stark reality of hunger that post-colonial India faces today. In the colonial period, the year 1866 was the darkest year in the history of Orissa. It was the year of the Great Famine that not only caused millions of starvation deaths, but also led to the erosion of the socio-moral values. While an inheritance of guilt still troubles him – grandfather walked into the folds of Christianity to keep his body and soul together – his son is not troubled as much, for there is the distance of time. In an attempt to find an answer to the grave Naxal problem he opines that he has become lopsided as his intellect fails. He remarks with a pathetic perspicacity:

> in the fiery violence of a revolutionary
> my reason becomes a prejudiced sorrow
> like socialism (29)

Such is the plight of India, the poet expresses his anguish over hunger dogging thousands of people in India. They are leading a wretched life. He remarks in "Trying to Keep Still":

> the wailing flutes burnt-out rice fields
> the heartbeats of children who have no fathers
> and the silence of one who calls himself God. (18)

The poet expresses dismay at the leaders' nonchalant attitude towards the fate of the common, poor people. He metaphorically says:

> Crows keep flying through fitful air
> but the spaces are empty, nothing fills them any more (18)

Thus Mahapatra identifies himself with the poor, down-trodden who are victims of the rich people, the self-centred leaders and the terrorists.

Another example of the unending violence appears when Graham Staines, an Australian missionary along with his two young sons were burnt alive on the night of January 22, 1999 in Orissa. In this context Mahapatra wrote:

> It was there, friend, this poem,
> its hands folded, eyes shut,
> looking down at those three charred corpses
> of a father and his two young sons
> in the middle of a long journey to nowhere.
> What it saw, turned to secret dust. (50)

In "Progress" where an Australian missionary and his two young sons were burnt alive. This poem is an effort of the poet to portray violence in its full nakedness as "It suffers from a frantic darkness" and this incident marked a stigma over the law and order of our country as if no one is safe in his / her home. The poet finds himself helpless in these kinds of situation as if "its hands folded, eyes shut" and to see what's all happening in and around him. That is exactly how he deals with the grim realities that surround himself and scream for attention. Not as a street-fighting activist who takes cudgels on behalf of the masses to pin down the system, but as a stoic, who sits on the border of events with the spirit of a conscious spectator.

Mahapatra's concern over the happenings of ruthless violence in the society in his recent volume in *Random Descent* depicting some ruins of the year 2002. The persistent tragic vision rolls before the poet's mind's eyes. A raped sixteen year old girl, a little girl's raped body, cries of women made hostages, a never ending scream of suffering and hatred, long speeches of the politicians, a maimed man, and a ruined country are the several subjects of these poems which portrays the existence of different kinds of violence in the society. The poet strongly says that this ruined land is not the land of his vision. He does not want to live in this land. He says:

The land some love to call holy
is not the one I want to live in.
Today the land of shrines and temples
offers its troubled tombs of blood,
when I don't want to write my poem,
while a mob watches, cheering in delight
at the sight of Fara's rape
and mutilation limb by limb. (70)

Thus the poet bravely declares his desires:

I want the graveyard to flower without its corpses,
and the sunlit street
to shine without its shadows.
I want the flames to warm the empty heart
of love, not burn a city with pitiable hatred.
I don't want to sit bent over a page
to reflect in it my griefs,
more for myself than for others.
I want my government to hover
like a butterfly over a garden;
not be, as it is, like a wasp or snake. (70)

Now, Mahapatra's poetry of non-comment turns to be the poetry of comment. It is the poetry voicing his protest and intolerance against the sufferings of the poor, weak and down trodden of the land. He wants to safeguard the poor sufferer and become their saviour. Therefore Mahapatra dwells on hunger, violence and terrorism. He judges political issues from the humanistic viewpoint. He depicts the predicament of human life at the same time presents the ghastly conditions of the society. He expresses his inability to discuss the violence of the extremists. He puts across his despairing attitude towards horror-ridden situation.

REFERENCES

1. Paranjape, Makarand., ed. Innerview, "Jayanta Mahapatra Talks to Makarand Paranjape." M. Sivaramakrishna March 1992. 13.

2. Das, Bijay Kumar. "A Critique of A Whiteness of Bone," *The Poetry of Jayanta Mahapatra*. New Delhi: Atlantic Publishers, 1995. 61.

3. Das, Bijay Kumar. "The Making of the Poet," *The Poetry of Jayanta Mahapatra*. 15.

4. Mahapatra, Jayanta. *Contemporary Author Autobiography Series*. 9. Michigan: 1989. 149.

5. Dwivedi, A. N. ed. "Shantiveer Kaul's Review of Firdaus in Flames in Indian Literature." Vol. XXXIX. No.2 March-April 1996. *Studies in Contemporary Indian English Drama* New Delhi: Kalyani Publishers, 1999.

6. Asif Currimbhoy on *The Bengal Triology* Cited in Inquilab. 2nd Ed. Calcutta: 1993. 4.

7. Nicholas Temasheff and George Thedorson, *Sociological Theory* quoted in Dwivedi, A. N. ed. *Studies in Contemporary Indian English Drama* New Delhi: Kalyani Publishers, 1999.

7

Conclusions

Jayanta Mahapatra is a major and representative modern Indian poet writing in English. Mahapatra's achievement is considerable with seventeen volumes of poetry (to date, including his *Selected Poems*), five volumes of Oriya poetry, eight volumes of poetry translations from Oriya to English, two volumes of stories, one book on Orissa and many articles in various journals, periodicals and newspapers. Also, Mahapatra's poetry very successfully reflects all the conflicts and tension of an Indian writing in English, of a Christian living in a Hindu society, and an intellectual living in a bewildering social setup undergoing a transformation at a fast phase from a rural and agrarian society to an industrialised and technological one.

Surprisingly such a writer has not been discussed seriously. There has been no full-length study of Jayanta Mahapatra's poetic output. There are some articles, reviews and short critical studies of individual poems / volumes of Mahapatra's poetry. The critical corpus on Mahapatra's poetry remains inadequate and therefore we see a compelling need for a comprehensive study of Jayanta Mahapatra's poetic world in order to understand both the poet and the time he is living in.

Infact, the oeuvre of Mahapatra can be considered in three distinct phases. In the early period, we see Mahapatra a novice in the act of writing poetry. *Close the Sky, Ten by Ten* and *Svayamvara and Other Poems*, the first two volumes of Mahapatra's poetry were published in 1971. Mahapatra's restless preoccupations with his characteristic poetic diction in its formative stage are quiet evident in these volumes. The poetry of this period reflects a lack of unified vision, what his early poetry communicates is a sense of inadequacy of his poetic equipment; i.e., language seems to be burdened with alogical abstractions, juxtaposition of contrasting images, etc. It often consists of a heap of images, which are self-contradictory in nature and this poses difficulty which puts off any reader. Unless one is repelled by the increasing obscurity of Mahapatra's poetic experience, the private symbolism and its significance may not be easily accessible to a reader. Therefore, in the early period, poetic expression often seem forced or inartistically contrived.

However, in *Svayamvara* we observe a move from the stage of arbitrariness and linguistic-obsession towards more concrete images and symbols. Simultaneously, many poems in this volume illustrate the shift in Jayanta Mahapatra's tone and attitude from a highly individualistic private symbolism towards a more general and contemporary social issues. In *A Father's Hours* (1976) Mahapatra attempts to carry out these intentions with much more conviction and convenience than in the preceding two volumes of his poetry. Moreover, instead of his usual preference for shorter poems, in *A Father's Hours* we see Mahapatra attempting to write longer poems which may be truly considered forerunners of his late single-poem volume *Relationship* and *Temple*. In *A Father's Hours* we also see his need to identify with the *Past*- cultural, social and individual and his inadequacy to belong to the *Present*. Infact, these preoccupations remain a long-drawn out obsession with Mahapatra, which manifests in all his later poetry in the form of recurrent themes and symbols.

A Rain of Rites (1976), *Waiting* (1979) and *The False Start* (1980) constitute the second phase of Mahapatra's poetic career which is marked by inventiveness and experimentation. *A Rain of Rites*, is Mahapatra's first book of poems published abroad and seems to be, a mature work both in terms of theme and structure. *Woman* is the substance of *A Rain of Rites*. The Indian womanhood by and large, is subject to all sorts of ill-treatment and suffering; and Mahapatra echoes this stark reality in all its nakedness. It is important to note that Mahapatra does not offer at obvious or probable solutions to the problems depicted in his poems, but leaves it to the better judgement of the reader. This neutral tone and distance from the experience of the poem are characteristic of Mahapatra's poetry.

Mahapatra's rumination over the past of Orissa, his need to belong to his place and his self-explorations in the cultural matrix of his social milieu form the nucleus of *Waiting*. In this volume, Mahapatra's quest for self-definition becomes more pronounced. Mahapatra digs up the sorrow, pain and suffering of the past which lie buried in the history of Orissa, and encounters them in his poetry. This, infact, defines the aesthetics and the nature of Mahapatra's poetic pursuits in general. Jayanta Mahapatra's search for meaning and significance of life takes him through a series of encounters between dream and reality in his next volume of poetry, *The False Start*. Here, we realise that Mahapatra's self-awareness is created by these encounters which are central to our understanding of Mahapatra's poetry. *The False Start* is, infact, a logical extension of all the major poetic concerns of Mahapatra that began with *Waiting*.

With the publication of *Relationship* (1980), Mahapatra enters the third phase of his poetic career marked by profound maturity of thought, sophisticated expression, deepening vision, contemplative mood and brooding tone.

Hence, Mahapatra's *Magnum Opus, Relationship* is the first long poem in twelve sections, which is profoundly philosophical and highly contemplative in nature. Mahapatra's *Relationship* is a poetic journey in space and time through the ruins of the once glorious Orissa and the ritualistic Tantrism invoking magic and myth of creation. Mahapatra lays great emphasis on the interactive influences of a cultured civilisation on man's eternal quest for *meaning and significance* of human existence. In this sense *Relationship* provides a satisfying experience which attempts at a unified vision.

In the next volume of his poetry *Life Signs* (1983), Mahapatra attempts to analyse the nature of his own creativity and its relevance. Here, Mahapatra tries to answer some valid and pertinent questions regarding his own inner world, doubts and convictions, which become the driving force of his poetry. *Life Signs* is thus of Mahapatra's uneven but eventful poetic path in which Mahapatra's soul-searching introspection to assess the way his poetry has evolved over the years proves to be an honest self-evaluation, and thus *Life Signs* is a stock taking as it were of Mahapatra's poetic endeavours.

In the next volume of his poetry *Dispossessed Nests: the 1984 Poems* (1986) is on the terrorism in Punjab and the Bhopal Gas Tragedy. This is the only poetry volume of Mahapatra, which is centred outside the Orissan landscape which otherwise is invariably at the core, forming an integral part of his poetry. Here, for once, the subject is lucid, real and familiar to the average readers and becomes readily understandable when seen against the general obscurity and opaqueness of Mahapatra's poetry in general. In its clarity, directness of thoughts, style and diction *Dispossessed Nests* differs from the rest of Mahapatra's poetry volumes.

With the publication of *Burden of Waves and Fruits* (1988) Mahapatra once again treads the familiar ground of his passionate obsession – Orissa. In this volume, Mahapatra broods over the burdens of his conscience which history of his land imposes on him. The deeply contemplative mood and the reflective tone help the poet to transform his burdens into a communicable experience. The central concerns of Mahapatra, infact, do not seem to indicate a linear progression; instead, what we see is a thematic concentration of human grief, sufferings, pain, loss, etc. from volume to volume. Hence, *Burden of Waves and Fruits* is yet another affirmation of Mahapatra's poetic pursuits.

Thematically, *Temple* (1989) is a continuation of *A Rain of Rites* published more than a decade earlier, in making *woman* the central character and the focus of Mahapatra's poetry. The progression of the theme gains in intensity and depth of treatment. Mahapatra captures, with rare insight, the burden of tradition on woman at all stages of their lives in the predominantly patriarchal system of our society. Chelammal, who in the ripe old age of 80, is to believe to have committed suicide along with her husband Ramanujan because of poverty and loneliness, becomes the guiding spirit of *Temple.* Chelammal echoes the dreams, disappointments and sighs of every Indian woman.

Temple is divided into three sections. In the first section, "The Hall of Dancing", Mahapatra introduces the reader to the subtleties of conventional man-woman bonding and depicts the buoyancy of feminine youthfulness. Mahapatra also portrays the subtle interplay of sexuality and poverty that shapes the lives of countless women in our country. In the second section, "The Hall of Offerings", Mahapatra depicts the second stage in the life of a woman when she offers herself to her man and sacrifices everything for the sake of her children. The third section, "Sanctum Sanctorum: The Shrine" is highly symbolic, invested with myths and legends. Here, the life of a woman comes full circle and she is redeemed through her own womanhood; the *legend of Putana* is effectively used to this end. Infact, Mahapatra uses the *Putana legend* as an extended metaphor for Indian women, as their redemption lies in their own womanhood.

A Whiteness of Bone was published in 1992. It may be rightly called the compendium of Mahapatra's poetic world because all his major thematic preoccupations find a place in this volume. Mahapatra's hesitations and doubts, confidence and affirmations and his ambivalent attitude to life, all manifest in the poem of *A Whiteness of Bone.* In this volume, Mahapatra seems to suggest that what is basically tragic alone inspires a poet to create something profound and authentic; and an unflinching endurance of suffering becomes a prerequisite for all creative endeavours and a true poet transports the essential human flaw and suffering into a lasting experience in his poetry.

The Best of Jayanta Mahapatra is a selection of best poems of Mahapatra published in 1995 from his book *A Rain of Rites* (1976) to *A Whiteness of Bone* (1992) and an autobiographical prose-fragment, edited by P.P. Raveendran, is considered to be the best representative selected work of Jayanta Mahapatra. In his introductory note, Raveendran highlights Mahapatra's act of decolonising Indian English Poetry: "Alone of all Indian poets writing with the possible exception of A.K. Ramanujan, it is in Jayanta Mahapatra's poetry, that this decolonising act takes on a quality and specificity comparable to the best verse written in Indian regional languages."

Shadow Space (1997) explains about the variegated ideas of helplessness, skepticism, superconsciousness, nostalgia, present reality, violence etc. Mahapatra becomes a grief stricken owing to his helplessness in a precarious predicament. Violence goes on a spree. The agitated mind smitten by painful thoughts and a note of mental peace often causes uncertainty in him. The poems in this volume very obviously step out on to the street and into the remote village, in order to express the poet's anguish about contemporary society. The inexplicable and ruthless violence and injustice of contemporary society has begun to worry the poet.

Bare Face (2000) is a collection of poems prefaced by Camilo Jose Cela's words, "A beheaded puppet is a sadder sight than a dead human being." In this collection Mahapatra is painfully aware of his past; memories, personal or as a legacy of burden, a journey backward through time in a dream-like state and of late Mahapatra's poetry has started assuming somewhat political overtones. In an article published in *The Hindu* Jayanta Mahapatra has ably dealt with the question. According to him, there cannot be any hard and fast rules, but poetry that ignore the historical relationship between the self and the society becomes lifeless.

Random Descent is Mahapatra's most recent collection of poetry published in the year 2005. In this volume his poetry of non-comment turns to be poetry of comment. It is the poetry voicing his protest and intolerance against the sufferings of the poor, weak and downtrodden of the land. He wants to safeguard the poor sufferer and the women class at large. Divided into three sections, this collection of poetry is a fresh recurrence of the old legends, the poet was elaborating throughout the past three decades, which deal with the familiar characteristic like Orissa's architectural cosmogony, social turmoils, widespread terrorism and Mahapatra's favourite images of stone, darkness and light emerge with renewed possibilities.

Mahapatra's poetry manifests his struggle with word-structures to create a meaning. Often a thought or an image or a mood starts him on his poetic voyage. He is led blindfold into a whirlpool of disturbing and recalcitrant realities in search of significance and meaning. The quest for appropriate alternatives- to transform his suffering and pain into pregnant images and metaphors- forms the nucleus of Mahapatra's constant pursuit.

Mahapatra's poetry registers his struggle with the resources of English language to create a meaningful expression. The quest for appropriate alternatives to transform his suffering and pain into potent images and metaphors forms the nucleus of Mahapatra's poetic pursuits. Jayanta Mahapatra invests his symbols with multiple meanings by compressing the images even when he deals with a concrete situation. Therefore, compression of images and distortion of phenomenal realities are Mahapatra's favourite techniques.

The dynamics of social behaviour often gets reflected in Jayanta Mahapatra's poetry. But he always avoids the dangerous approach of a political philosopher or a social reformer. Mahapatra is content only to reflect the complex nature of the forces operating in the society and the predicament of the individual caught in the web of all these forces. This is most significant characteristic of Mahapatra's poetry as it avoids the reductionist view of man's eternal struggle by over-simplification.

In Mahapatra deeply felt experiences are internalised which sink deep into the layers of his subconsciousness, undergo a dramatic metamorphosis, and surface unexpectedly in disguised forms in his poetry. Jayanta Mahapatra is a poet of abstractions, paradoxes and internal conflicts which are his modes of perception. Hence, Mahapatra's poetry defies all attempts at paraphrasing and at best conveys the uncertainty of human life which results in a sense of restlessness. This accounts for the obscurity we encounter in Mahapatra's poetry, which impair effective communication between the poet and his readers. Paul Valery says that it is the reading of the poem that is the poem. This is especially true of Jayanta Mahapatra's poetry. Here, the reader often confronts a body of poetry which resists being highly subjective in nature, often incoherent, defying logic and even simple rules of grammar and syntax. Therefore, Mahapatra's poetry is addressed to a discriminating reader – a *sahrudaya* – who is willing to take pains to encounter the experience held captive within the structure of the poem. The readers' own experience should guide them to unravel the mysteries of Mahapatra's poetic creation. Thus, in Mahapatra we see a generous invitation for reader involvement in the experience of the poem. In Mahapatra's poetry, the primacy of reader-response is as much valid as the primacy of the text itself. Mahapatra's poetry does not give any message to its readers in the form of a well-phrased witticism. Instead, it makes the reader look inwards, question himself about life, its significance, uncertainty and so on leading him into a process of personal discovery. This indeed is a great strength of Mahapatra's poetry.

The coexistence of Life and Death, Absurdity and Meaningfulness, Good and Evil – a pair of opposites – bears a tremendous significance for Mahapatra, because one has meaning only in relation to the other. Mahapatra is aware of this manifestation of duality as the law of Nature and his poetry communicates the pulls of unresolved oppositions. Hence, simultaneity of contrasting experience and perceptions becomes the shaping force of Mahapatra's poetry. From the concrete to the abstract, from the ruins of history – the temples of Konarka and the Kalinga War – to the glorious past of Orissa, Mahapatra's probing spirit wanders in search of *Meaning* that would lead to self-realisation. Hence, Mahapatra's poetry is essentially self-exploratory in nature.

In his poetry, Mahapatra uses certain images and symbols in his poetry like *death, darkness, past, silence, door, etc.,* which become the recurrent motifs of his poetry. Mahapatra's poetry volumes are held in closer relationship by the recurrence of these motifs, as well as by their thematic repetitiveness, which give unity and significance to Mahapatra's modes of perceiving an experience rooted either in the reality of the external world or the interior landscape of his poetic imagination. Mahapatra's poetry is an attempt to relate himself to his environment, to the socio-cultural milieu of his land – Orissa and its history, both ancient and modern. His poetry defines his ways of belonging to what is contemporary in society and what is permanent and elusive in the eternal flux of time, which become the generative force of Mahapatra's poetry.

Death is a recurring dominant theme in Mahapatra's poetic world. Fear of death guides the poet back to life, urging him to live more vigorously and more meaningfully. Mahapatra knows that Death and Life are not two unrelated abstractions. They are not only complementary but one has significance only in relation to the other and together they complete the cyclical process in Nature. Death, infact, has been a major theme in contemporary Indian poetry in English. For example, Keki N. Daruwalla's depiction of death has the serenity of calm acceptance as an inevitable natural order of events. Whereas Mahapatra's treatment of death gains in intensity and depth by its rich suggestiveness as a cyclical process with the much desired powers. A. K. Ramanujan, for instance, does not brood over death guides them back to life; but, in Ramanujan, the impact of death on the living becomes more important as it gets reflected in the social behaviour of those near and dear to the dead; whereas in Mahapatra's poetry death renews man's zeal for a more meaningful living.

Darkness becomes an early childhood fixation in Mahapatra's life which projects into his poetry almost as a neurotic obsession symbolising the fear of unknown, anxiety, uncertainty, hatred, helplessness, a sense of entrapment, impotent rage and a host of other negative feelings, this pervading darkness makes the poet acutely aware of himself, his limitations, frustrations and failures. *Darkness* sharpens Mahapatra's sensitivity though it only results in pain and despair; and he dwells in the world of darkness with his archaic despair willingly. Darkness, thus, becomes Mahapatra's meditative ground which directs him to look inwards. Mahapatra offers a wide spectrum of darkness for self-introspection providing diverse points of view.

Mahapatra attempts to enrich life by giving meaning and purpose through an encounter with the Past, which in his case, is the past of the once-glorious Orissa. Mahapatra strongly believes that his present is only an extension of the past, and has its roots in the past which is not lost in time. Therefore, in Mahapatra's poetry there is a constant attempt to relate the two worlds – the past and the present – in order that each may trigger a response which the other reciprocates, together forming an unbroken Time-continuum. Self- awareness is born as a result of his poetic voyage back and forth in time. *Past* thus becomes the shaping influence in Mahapatra's poetry. Hence, Mahapatra's personal destiny is thus inseparably linked with the destiny of his land.

Any significant change generally has an unpleasant past, or a painful history. New awareness is born, like the proverbial Phoenix, out of the accumulated pain, sorrow and misery of the past. Mahapatra realises this in the specific context of the disastrous Kalinga War which brought in its wake untold agony, loss, deprivation and despair; yet the ravages of the War so moved Emperor Asoka that he turned to the compassionate teachings of the Buddha and helped to promote Buddhism in the far east. Mahapatra's acknowledges his debt to such a past which shapes one's life. In Mahapatra's poetry the past evolves as a conscious, constructive and evaluative presence, which renders Mahapatra a significant poet among his contemporaries in Indian poetry in English.

Silence is eloquent in Mahapatra's poetry. It is rendered qualitative because it guides both the poet and the reader to meditate on the quality of human life. Hence, silence is not a state of speechlessness but becomes creative and meaningful. In the poetry of Jayanta Mahapatra, silence represents what is lost in a culture by the onslaught of modernity and also the mystery of the past. Mahapatra uses silence as a symbol of the unattainable, unknowable, and the inexplicable that has an undeniably strong presence in the life of all human beings: it leads man on his eternal quest for meaning, an element that renders quality to all human activities in the face of uncertainty, frustration and gloom. Mahapatra's poetry depicts a dominant father-figure image, father-son relationship becomes symbolic but defiantly rejects their shared heritage. We may recall here that Mahapatra's grandfather was a Hindu who embraced Christianity during the terrible famine which struck Orissa in 1866. Mahapatra's parents became staunch Christians and as a child Mahapatra "had a rigid Christian upbringing". Mahapatra's denial of the father's world – the newly embraced faith (Christianity) – comes more as an assertion of the Hindu roots than rejecting the new faith as inferior. This is an important observation in understanding Mahapatra's dilemma of a divided inheritance neither of which he can accept or reject fully.

Therefore, an ambivalent approach to life and its problem becomes characteristic of Mahapatra's poetry.

Door is a significant motif in Mahapatra's poetry which keeps haunting him right through the painful days of childhood. The door becomes a symbol of suffocating captivity and confinement, a fearsome prison of body and mind. The door makes Mahapatra aware of his own helplessness. Now in the adult world, every time he passes a door, what he encounters there is his own self, *the other within*, the other unknown till then. This becomes an endless game of hide and seek, recognition and disbelief, affirmation and negation, which is frightening and reassuring at the same time, appearing as a bundle of contradictions – that is essentially Mahapatra's unique mode of perception.

Time is the *leit motif* in the poetry of Jayanta Mahapatra. Mahapatra's poetic vision is projected in time-pattern or a time-scheme; it ranges from the minuscule to eternity. It makes an attempt to study how Mahapatra explores the metaphoric interiority of time in his poetry. It advances that Mahapatra's concepts of time, which is neither rectilinear nor circular or cyclical, emerges from the nature of his own existence, both as a human being and as a poet, constantly being confronted by morality-immorality and flux-permanence dialectics.

Jayanta Mahapatra's poetry is essentially metaphorical in nature. His language of poetry chooses for itself a different lexicon to depict the socio-cultural ambience of Orissa by the experiencing-self of the poet. While it is true that Mahapatra deliberately chooses to dislocate his subjective experience in the mosaic of mixed metaphors in his poetry, he also endows it with rich resonances which yield to multiple interpretations. Rain is one such significant metaphor which gets endlessly repeated in

Mahapatra's poetry. For Mahapatra, rain becomes both the destroyer and the saviour of mankind. There are references to the rain that has lost its regenerative power, and the rain brings in the much-desired expiation and atonement. Therefore, the metaphoric mode in the image-oriented poetry of Mahapatra becomes the nucleus of his creative endeavours.

It is not surprising that in the highly subjective poetry of Jayanta Mahapatra, ironic mode of expression is neither a dominant nor a preferred poetic device. It is only in his recent poetry volumes that we get to hear a shade of Mahapatra's ironic voice. Mahapatra's irony is not a pungent remark or a comment and is never biting, bitter or sharp, never borders on sarcasm or takes cover under witty statements. Daruwalla's biting sarcasm and devastating irony provide a perfect contrast to Mahapatra's style. Irony in Mahapatra's poetry is always subdued, a self-talk that invariably leads to self-introspection, being directed more towards himself, focusing his own limitations and shortcomings as a man and poet. "A Missing Person", "Hunger", "The Whorehouse in a Calcutta Street", "30th January 1982: A Story" and "The Twentyfifth Anniversary of a Republic: 1975" are the classic examples of Mahapatra's poetry *as social commitment*. Here, we may observe how irony, though mute in the characteristic style of Mahapatra, renders an intensity and immediacy to the experience handled in the specific contexts of his poetry. This clearly shows the shift Mahapatra's poetry has taken from a highly subjective world towards articulating problems that concern the people at large.

Mahapatra was twice removed from his immediate surroundings – first, he was born into a Christian family in a predominantly Hindu society and second, he wrote in an acquired medium, English, which was considered not adequate to encompass the cultural spirit of his native land. Yet the themes which dominate his poetry are related to such stark realities of India as hunger, myths, rituals, sexuality, spirituality, the self and eternity. His poetry, whether describing the locale, its environs and landscape or the relationship of his self to his land, attempts to reflect an awareness of this milieu. It aims at evaluating Mahapatra as the Mouth-Piece of India in the perspective of the locale, in terms of the images drawn from the geographical, social and cultural sources of his native land of Orissa. The place with all its ethos and myths, its lives and beliefs, superstitions and transitions has been the governing factor of his (poet) perceptions and vision but at the same time it's having a national appeal too. Mahapatra has repeatedly and candidly said that when he started writing poetry, his knowledge of poetry did not go beyond a few poems of Wordsworth, Keats and Shelley prescribed in the school syllabus. At heart he is a romantic; only his intellect sharpened by the profession of teaching physics won't let him indulge in it. In his poetry one feels the presence of "the still, sad music of humanity" of Wordsworth, the sweeping lyrical grace of Shelley and the sensuousness of Keats. He has always remained close to the Romantic notion of the poet's inescapable presence in the poem; it nevertheless embodies in such a self a deep subjectivity that sets it apart from contemporary Indian poetry in English.

This element of subjectivity helped him to relate himself to his milieu and landscape in a delicate way never done before in Indian English poetry. The exploration of the inner self is intricately woven with his childhood experiences as much with the Oriya fairy tales, myths and legends. Along with these sources close to his locale, he updated himself with a voracious reading of modern classics of the world as well as contemporary writings in scores of established periodicals like *The Sewanee review, The Hudson Review, The Kenyon Review, The Times Literary*

Supplement, Critical Quarterly, Poetry where he himself published profusely. It is the Oriya sensibility as well as the lyrical quality of traditional Oriya poetry which provides charm and grace to his poetry. The tight-knit family life, the rites and rituals associated with the cyclic agricultural seasons, the rich tradition of arts and crafts and an easy, quiet pace of life are some of the major Orissan elements that recur in terms motifs, images and symbols.

The Orissa landscape – with Puri and Konark looming large – has a strong presence in the poetry of Mahapatra. But more than the physical surroundings, it is the deeper levels of Indianness that are crucial. The tone of quiet acceptance, with a latent awareness of centuries of sufferings, perhaps indicates a very Indian sensibility. The cadence sound very Indian, and are apparently shaped by such influences as Mahapatra's father reading from the epics in the poet's childhood. Mahapatra has said of himself that he is "an Oriya poet who incidentally writes in English," and that, for all he cares, his Poems may be read as "translations". Indeed Mahapatra effortlessly 'translates' a profoundly Indian spirit into English; No other Indian English poet appears to have succeeded to the same extent in that difficult task. His poetry also displays the working of an extremely sensitive, supple imagination. Mahapatra, apart from being highly locale and international, is also very individual. No other English poet approaches the depth, the sweep and the subtlety of Mahapatra's imagination. Much of the Mahapatra's poetry is difficult, if not impossible, to paraphrase.

More than any other Indian English poet, Mahapatra depends upon the resources of the un-conscious, and his un-conscious would seen to connect more than most with the collective un-conscious of India.

Myths are the potent symbols of man's dreams and aspirations. Mankind's history is codified in its myths and therefore myths symbolically represent what has stirred man's soul in his life's journey from times immemorial. Jayanta Mahapatra attempts to penetrate into the hidden depths of the collective unconsciousness of human race by breaking through the mythical heritage of man. By correlating with man's eternal preoccupations Mahapatra endeavours to define the predicament of modern man torn between conflicting values, shattered faiths, and a near-total absence of life-sustaining mythical values. Myths operate at two levels – social and cultural – in Mahapatra's poetry. At either level, myths undergo a metamorphosis to bring into focus the present degradation and debasement of human life and its consequent loss of enduring quality. In the modern context, myths are stripped bare and they serve as poor travesty of their original rich symbolic suggestiveness. Hence, we experience the deglorification and sometimes even the debunking of myths in Mahapatra's poetry.

Mouth as a recurrent image symbolises the denial of mythic dimension to the quests of modern man both at the cultural and social level. For Mahapatra, the mythic process becomes wearisome and weighs heavily because the mental preparedness of people to rejuvenate their cultural sources is hard to come by. Therefore, Mahapatra feels that the ideal of human happiness remains a myth. Mahapatra also shatters the myth of unified India by his realistic portrayal of our society in the light of religious intolerance, fanaticism, fundamentalism, corrupt atmosphere of displaced loyalties and secessionist tendencies. So myths have ceased to be functional. Mahapatra feels it ridiculous that women are subjected to all sorts of ill-treatment in a country which abounds in mythical allusions elevating women to be the status of a goddess and mother. In the heart of all these mythical allusions for example, burden of chastity and *Laxman-rekha*, Mahapatra hears a lurking presence of the stifled cry for help and the shame of the wronged woman. Mahapatra feels that equality of sexes and dignity of the human person very largely remains a myth even to this day.

In, *Relationship*, Mahapatra deals with the *Myth of Origin*, i.e., myth of origin of this Universe and the myth of origin of man on this planet. Mahapatra's explorations into the Myths of Origin are rooted in the non-Vedic derivative of Indian culture in the form of Tantrism with its supreme emphasis on the Female Principle (*Prakriti*). The union of *Prakriti* with *Purusha* or the Male Principle brings forth the Cosmic creation in its entirety. Mahapatra depicts this Tantric cosmogony brilliantly in *Relationship*. No doubt such a cosmogony is primitive, yet the fact that it was rooted in the agricultural magic and the fertility cult, proves the centrality of sexual rites in Tantrism and Mahapatra utilises the suggestive power of this cult to celebrate life forces. It is only natural that Mahapatra is influenced by the Tantric motifs because Orissa was once the seat of widespread Tantric cult. Mahapatra stresses that the quests of our Tantric ancestors should not be dismissed as a perverted system of rites, because their emphasis on the *Deha Tattva* (cult of the body) certainly paved the way for the development of scientific spirit of enquiry into the nature of things.

The most curious and significant feature to be observed in Mahapatra's poetic world is his inability to maintain relationship either with his wife Runu Mahapatra, whom he loved and married against stiff opposition from his parents, which eventually led Mahapatra to leave the house of his parents and set up his own home or his mother with whom his relationship was also not comfortable but he still looked after her till her death in 2003.

Mahapatra expresses his anguish and angst about the degenerate values which have seeped into the contemporary life of the country. Self-centeredness of people and leaders looms large in the nations politics which ultimately is one of the examples of growing materialism in the society. Moreover, partisan outlook and debased moral values have despoiled the country of its image. Mahapatra also portrays the whole ambience of violence and destruction. Each draw begins with a night-marish experience to men, women and children. Hence God's dreams of steering the universe in an orderly way are blighted and shattered. The reverse side of the universe, that is the world, is drowned in darkness. So the violence is the order of the day. Violence has spread in every nook and cranny except over the foothills. No protest against violence is noticed. The poet decries meaningfulness of silence – silence which is distinguishable from the silence of beatitude. He also denounces people who escape for fear of violence shedding their courage and bravery to fight terrorism. These cowards are living a life of silence. He condemns the escapists.

Also, Mahapatra does not lose touch with his native tradition. He is also involved with contemporary society by watching its ways from close quarters. He does not run away from realities of life but faces them with courage and conviction. His poetry is authentic of lives and people described in it. His characters are real people in flesh and blood whom we met in our daily life. He has written about Bhopal Gas Tragedy, the Gulf War, Riots of Bombay in 1994, the Kalahandi starvation deaths, the anti-national activities in Punjab in the name of Khalistan, the Murder of Indira Gandhi, the Naxalite movements and an Australian missionary along with his two young sons were burnt alive in Orissa etc., are related to various political and social problems that India is facing today. Living amid Corruption, Violence, Poverty, Indiscipline and Hunger of his people, Mahapatra has learnt how to flow down like a river to the throats of ancestral past in quest of solace and in search of his roots. This solemnity, this meditated humility makes Mahapatra a home-bound pilgrim, an instinctive insider. He himself questions the validity of his writing poetry whether it has done anything to change the society.

Essential social values of peace, universal brotherhood, love, and patriotism no longer evoke a positive response; anybody who proclaims to be the harbinger of such values is looked upon with suspicion. Religion has ceased to be cohesive force binding people together, and in its place religious intolerance, fanaticism and fundamentalism raise their ugly heads. What is shocking is that we have blindly come to passively accept these perversions as natural. We seems to be addicted to violence and hatred. Mahapatra grieves over man's distorted values and its impact on the younger generations, which grows in the corrupt atmosphere of displaced loyalties and secessionist tendencies.

Therefore, a glance at his poem reveals Mahapatra's angst over violence preempting non-violence in the society. He bemoans terrorism stalking in Punjab and depicts how non-violence is on death-bed and is surviving on glucose displays the feeble structure of the society. The terrorist movement is spawned in liaison with the government. The poet throws a trenchant remark against the culpable government. Thus Mahapatra identifies himself with the poor, down-trodden who are victims of the rich people, the self-centred leaders and the terrorists.

It is a fact that every literary work is the product of its Time – historical, social and geographical – which defines the choice of subjects, themes, modes of perception and articulation and the ways of responding to a literary work. Even creative writer faces these challenges in his own ways. In order to see how Mahapatra responds to these specific challenges, we may draw parallels from the poetic concerns of Edwin Thumboo – an eminent poet of

Singapore. For Thumboo, identity-crisis becomes the most important aspect of his poetry, which, in the greater context, becomes truly representative of the need of all Singaporeans. But for Mahapatra, the need to belong to his specific socio-cultural milieu by identifying with the destiny and the ethos of Orissa alone consumes a life-time of poetic pursuits. Thus, Thumboo and Mahapatra represent the different ways in which poets respond to the challenges of their socio-cultural demands.

Jayanta Mahapatra's broad spectrum of poetry demonstrates the gradual evolution of the poet from the initial stages of experimentation with the English language against the backdrop of the Orissan milieu, culture and history, to the level of finding a personal idiom and accomplishment of sophisticated linguistic skills, with an equally resonant personal voice and an individuality of his own. All his poetry, is therefore an intricate journey into the self. It is truly a rewarding encounter for the poet in particular and for the readers in general.

Bibliography

Primary Sources

Poetry:

Mahapatra, Jayanta. *Close the Sky, Ten by Ten.* Calcutta: Dialogue Publication, 1971.

Mahapatra, Jayanta. *Svayamvara and Other Poems.* Calcutta: Writers Workshop, 1971.

Mahapatra, Jayanta. *A Father's Hours.* Calcutta. Untied Writers, 1976.

Mahapatra, Jayanta. *A Rain of Rites.* Athens: The University of Georgia Press, 1976.

Mahapatra, Jayanta. *Waiting.* New Delhi: Samkaleen Prakashan, 1979.

Mahapatra, Jayanta. *The False Start.* Bombay: Clearing House, 1980.

Mahapatra, Jayanta. *Relationship.* New York: The Green field Review Press, 1980.

Mahapatra, Jayanta. *Life Signs.* New Delhi: Oxford University Press, 1983.

Mahapatra, Jayanta. *Dispossessed Nests: The 1984 Poems.* Jaipur: Nirala Publications, 1986.

Mahapatra, Jayanta. *Selected Poems.* New Delhi: Oxford University Press, 1987.

Mahapatra, Jayanta. *Burden of Waves and Fruits: Poems.* Washington, D.C. Three Continents Press, 1988.

Mahapatra, Jayanta. *Temple.* Sidney: Dangaroo Press, 1989.

Mahapatra, Jayanta. *A Whiteness Of Bone.* New Delhi: Viking, Penguin Books India Private Ltd., 1992.

Mahapatra, Jayanta. *The Best of Jayanta Mahapatra.* Kozikode: Bodhi Publishers, 1995.

Mahapatra, Jayanta. *Shadow Space.* Kottayam: D.C. Books, 1997.

Mahapatra, Jayanta. *Bare Face.* Kottayam: D.C. Books, 2001.

Mahapatra, Jayanta. *Random Descent.* Bhubaneshwar: Third Eye Communications, 2005.

Literary Essays, Journals and Articles:

"About Hunger and Myself." *Keynote* 1 March 1982.

"Face to Face with the Contemporary Poem." *Journal of Literary Studies* 6. 1-2 June 1983.

"Letter from India." *The Poetry Review* 1.2 1984.

"Slow Swim in Dim Light: Quest for Modernity in Poetry." *The Bombay Review,*1, 1991, 5-11.

"The Measure of Mystery in Poetry." *Journal of Literary Studies,* 10.1, 1987.

"The Poet's Blues." *Youth Times* 7.17 February 1-14, 1980.

"The Stranger Within: Coming to Terms through Poetry." *The Dalhousie Review,* 63.3, Autumn 1983.

Secondary Sources

Books:

Alexander, Meena. *The Poetic Self.* New Delhi: Arnold Heinemann, 1979.

Amanuddin, Syed. *World Poetry in English.* New Delhi: Sterling Publication House, 1981.

Ameeruddin, Syed. *Indian Verse in English.* Madras: Poet Press India, 1977.

Bhatnagar, O.P. and R.A. Joshi: *Indian Poetry in English:* Old and New Jaipur: Rachana Publication, 1989.

Camus, Albert, *The Myth of Anxiety. Trans.* Justin O' Brien. NewYork: Vintage 1995.

Daruwalla, Keki. N. ed. *Two Decades of Indian Poetry: 1960-1980.* New Delhi: Vikas Publication, 1980.

Das, Bijay Kumar. *Critical Essays on Poetry.* New Delhi: Kalyani Publishers, 1993.

Das, Bijay Kumar. *Modern Indo-English Poetry.* Bareilly: Prakash Book Depot, 1982.

Das, Bijay Kumar. *Perspectives of Indian English Poetry Criticism.* Bareilly: Prakash Book Depot, 1993.

Das, Bijay Kumar. *The Poetry of Jayanta Mahapatra.* New Delhi: Atlantic Publishers, 1995.

Dwivedi, A.N. *Studies in Contemporary Indo-English Verse.* Bareilly: Prakash Book Depot, 1984.

Dwivedi, A.N., *Studies in Contemporary Indo-English Poets.* Bareilly: Prakash 1984.

Kantak, V.Y. *Perspectives on India Literary Culture.* New Delhi: Pencraft International, 1996.

Kermode, Frank. *Poetry, Narrative, History* Britain: Basil Balckwell, 1990.

King, Bruce. *Modern Indian Poetry in English.* New Delhi: Oxford University Press, 1987.

Lall, Emmanuel Narendra. *The Poetry of Encounter. Three Indo-Anglian Poets.* New Delhi: Sterling Publication House, 1983.

Mohan, Devinder. *Jayanta Mahapatra.* New Delhi: Arnold Heinemann, 1987.

Naik, M.K. *Perspectives on Indian Poetry in English,* New Delhi: Abhinav Prakashan, 1984.

Padhi, Saroj Kumar. *Jayanta Mahapatra's Relationship: A Critical Study*. Bareilly: Prakash Book Depot, 1997.

Panikar, Ayyappa K. *Indian Literature Since Independence.* Madras: Anu Chitra, 1989.

Panikar, Ayyappa K. ed. *Indian Literature Independence.* New Delhi: Indian Association for English Studies, 1990.

Paranjape, Makarand. ed. *Indian Poetry in English*. Madras: Macmillan India Ltd., 1993.

Parthasarthy, R. ed. *Ten Twentieth Century Indian Poets.* New Delhi: Oxford University Press 1986.

Pathak, R.S. *Quest for Identity*. New Delhi: Bahri Publication, 1992.

Prasad, Hari Mohan. *Indian Poetry in English*. Aurangabad: Parimal 1983.

Prasad, Madhusudan. *Living Indian English Poets: An Anthology of Critical Essays* New Delhi: Sterling Publication House, 1989.

Raghunandan, Laxmi. *Contemporary Indian Poetry in English.* New Delhi: Reliance, 1990.

Raveendran, P.P. ed. *The Best of Jayanta Mahapatra.* Kozikode: Bodhi Publishers, 1995.

Shahane, Vasant A. and M. Sivaramkrishnan, *Indian Poetry in English: A Critical Assessment*. New Delhi: Macmillan India Ltd., 1980.

Singh, Amar Kumar. *Enlightening Studies in Indian English Poetry*. Delhi: Manak, 1993.

Singh, R.K. *Indian English Writing 1981-1985: Experiments with Expressions*. New Delhi: Bahri Publication, 1987.

Sinha, K.N. ed. *Indian Writing in English*. NewDelhi: Heritage 1979.

Literary Essays, Journals and Articles:

Alexander, Meena., ed. *"A Poetry of Decreation" The Poetry of Jayanta Mahapatra: A Critical Study*. Madhusudan Prasad, New Delhi: Sterling Publication House, 1986. 132-39.

Ameeruddin, Syed., ed. *"Monika Varma" Studies in Contemporary Indo-English verse: A Collection of Critical Essays on Female Poets*. A.N. Dwivedi. Bareilly: Prakash Book Depot, 1984:182-93.

Bhatnagar, O.P., ed. *"The Indian Poetry in English: The Contemporary Situation" Studies in Indo-English Verse: A Collection of Critical Essays on Male Poets*. A.N. Dwivedi, Bareilly: Prakash Book Depot, 1984:10-19.

Chitre, Dilip. *"Poetry in the Enemy tongue" New Quest* 14 Jan-Feb. 1979. 77-82.

Das, Bijay Kumar. "Journey into the unknown Jayanta Mahapatra's *Relationship" The Humanities Review* 5. 1983, 5-7.

David, P.C., ed. "The Concept of Time in *The False Start" The Poetry of Jayanta Mahapatra*. Madhusudan Prasad, 1986. 115-31

Debydeen, Cyril. "Telephone Message for Mr. Jayanta Mahapatra: A Memoir" *World Literature Written in English* 32.1 Spring 1992. 88-95.

Devy, G.N., ed. "The Landscape of return." *The Poetry of Jayanta Mahapatra*. Madhusudan Prasad. 1986. 140-52.

Dutta, Ujjal., ed. "Some Animadversion." *The Poetry of Jayanta Mahapatra*. Madhusudan Prasad, 1986. 277-89.

Jayaprada, C.L.L. "Jayanta Mahapatra, the poet." *The Commonwealth Review* 5.2 1993-94: 86-91.

Kennedy, Alan., ed. "Written Rites." *The Poetry of Jayanta Mahapatra*. Madhusudan Prasad. 1986.74-97.

Khan, M.Q. "Jayanta Mahapatra Review of the Poetry of Jayanta Mahapatra." *The Literary Half-Yearly* 38.1 January 1997. 137-39.

King, Bruce. "Experimentalists: Mehrotra and Mahapatra. "*Modern Indian Poetry in English*. New Delhi: Oxford University Press, 1987. 183-208.

King, Bruce., ed. "The Shapes of Solitude. "*The Poetry of Jayanta Mahapatra*. Madhusudan Prasad. 1986. 1-23.

Kohli, Devinder. Quoted "Landscape and poetry. *The Journal of Commonwealth Literature,* 13.3 April 1979.

Love, Paul. "An Orissa Odyssey: Review Article". *Kavya Bharati* 5 1993.109-13.

Mahapatra, Sitakant. "Immediacy and Relevance. "*Indian Verse*. 5.1 Winter 1997: 9-12.

Mohanty, Niranjan., ed. "Dialectics of Love". *The Poetry of Jayanta Mahapatra: A Critical Study*. Madhusudan Prasad. 1986. 237-49.

Mohanty, Niranjan. "Pattern in Awareness: A Study in *Relationship.*" *Literary Criterion* 15. 1-2 June-December 1989. 44-56.

Mohanty, Niranjan. "Quest for Roots: Poetry of Jayanta Mahapatra." *Creative Forum* 5.1-4 January-Dec. 1989. 110-20.

Mohanty, Niranjan. "Sex, Power and Beyond: A Study in the Poetry of Jayanta Mahapatra." *The Quest* 1.1 March 1987. 36-54.

Mohanty, Niranjan., ed. "The Theme-Song of Life. Poetry of Jayanta Mahapatra." *Contemporary Indo-English Poetry*. Bijay Kumar Das. Bareilly: Prakash Book Depot, 1986. 64-86.

Mohanty, Niranjan. Recollection as Redemption: Poetry of Jayanta Mahapatra" *Poetry* 10. 1985. 24-40.

Naik, M.K., ed. "Landscape and Inscapes." *Kavya Bharati* 1. Jayanta Mahapatra Madurai: American College, 1989. 65-71.

Naik, M.K., ed. "The Two Worlds of Imagery." *The poetry of Jayanta Mahapatra* Madhusudan Prasad 1986. 98-114.

Paranjape, Makarand. "Introduction." *Indian Poetry in English,* Madras: Macmillan India Ltd., 1993. 1-27.

Perry, John Oliver., ed. Approaching Jayanta Mahapatra's *Temple" Framing Literature:* Critical Essays. B. Rama Nair, Gopal Rao and D. Venketeshwarulu. New Delhi: Sterling Publication House. 1995. 75-89.

Prasad, Hari Mohan. "A Study in Culture, Language and Tradition." Indian Poetry in English. Aurangabad: Parimal, 1983: 1-23.

Prasad, S.N. "Quest for Roots in the Poetry of Jayanta Mahapatra. " *The Journal of Indian Writing in English* 17.1 Jan 1989. 22-32.

Raina, M.L. "Interrogating the Myths. Review of *Relationship."* *Indian Book Chronical.* 6.19 Oct. 1, 1981. 326-27.

Ramkrishnan, E.V., ed. "Landscape as Destiny: Jayanta Mahapatra's Poetry." *Contemporary Indo-English Poetry.* B.K. Das. Bareilly: Prakash Book Depot, 1986: 102-10.

Rath, Harihar. "Life against Ruins: A Study of Jayanta Mahapatra's *The False Start."* Indian Scholar 3.1 Jan 1981. 85-92.

Reuben, Elizabeth. "*Relationship*. Book Review." The Indian P.E.N. 47. 5-6 May-June 1985. 18-21.

Shahane, Vasant A., ed. "*Relationship*: A Study in Myth: *The Poetry of Jayanta Mahapatra.* Madhusudan Prasad 1986. 168-80.

Stachniewski, John. "Review Article: *Life Signs* in the Poetry of Jayanta Mahapatra." *The Indian Literary Review* 26.2 April 1986: 79-84.

Sundari, G. and K.S. Ramamurthy., ed. "Song of the Past." *The Poetry of Jayanta Mahapatra*. Madhusudan Prasad. 1986. 153-67.

Swain, Rabindra K., ed. "A Voice of Humility: Poetry of Jayanta Mahapatra." *Indian Literature*. Keshav Malik. 26.1 1983. 79-87.

Swain, Rabindra K. "The Man, the Place and the Poet." *Indian Horizons* 41.4 1992. 37-47.

Swain, Rabindra K., ed. "Uncovering Lost Possibilities." *The Poetry of Jayanta Mahapatra*. Madhusudan Prasad. 2002. 265-76.

Swain, Rabindra K. "Review of The Best of Jayanta Mahapatra": *Indian Literature*. Vol. 179. May-June 1997. 191-193.

Syal, Pushpinder., ed. "The Use of Language." *The Poetry of Jayanta Mahapatra* Madhusudan Prasad. 1986. 198-219.

Index

***